# Keeping Good Employees On Board
## *Employee Retention Strategies to*
## *Navigate Any Economic Storm*

*Barbara,*
*Smooth Sailing,*
*Dawn*

# Keeping Good Employees On Board
## *Employee Retention Strategies to Navigate Any Economic Storm*

Dawn McCooey, M.A.

New York

# Keeping Good Employees On Board
## Employee Retention Strategies to Navigate Any Economic Storm

ISBN 978-1-60037-654-2

Library of Congress Control Number: 2009929151

# MORGAN · JAMES
### THE ENTREPRENEURIAL PUBLISHER

Morgan James Publishing, LLC
1225 Franklin Ave., STE 325
Garden City, NY 11530-1693
Toll Free 800-485-4943
www.MorganJamesPublishing.com

Habitat for Humanity® Peninsula Building Partner

In an effort to support local communities, raise awareness and funds, Morgan James Publishing donates one percent of all book sales for the life of each book to Habitat for Humanity. Get involved today, visit www.HelpHabitatForHumanity.org.

# Acknowledgements

Many people have contributed their knowledge and expertise to this project, helping me to structure my experiences and findings into this book. Thank you, Julie Salisbury for your inspiration; to Bliss Cochran, talented editor and fellow sailor, thank you for all of your help with the details; Margo Toulouse editor and guide; to my daughter, Mariah who provided not only encouragement, but with her journalist's eye, helped me to shape the book into its current form.

I am indebted to all of the kind people heading organizations that distributed my survey (listed in appendices); sincere thanks to the amazing employers who shared their stories (also listed in appendices). To my children, Mariah, Chris and Sam, sailors all, my deepest, resounding appreciation for who you are and for your collective encouragement and support. And the best for last… my husband, Pat, my captain and soul mate, I will sail to the ends of the earth with you.

# Contents

# Preface

I have an intense passion about the subject of employee retention, fueled by an insatiable curiosity about why some organizations have low employee turnover, while others struggle. This book explores the issues of employee retention from the employer perspective, and provides some insight and practical examples from employers who are practicing those leadership skills that contribute to success in maintaining employees in this volatile labor market.

As part of the research process for this book, I compiled the results of a survey from 525 employees, 70 percent of whom had quit a job within the past five years. I distributed the survey to unemployed persons who had accessed employment and career service centers in Canada. This data is not empirical research, but nonetheless provides some insight into the reasons that people leave jobs and what it is that makes them stay.

I got the employer perspective through interviews with success-story employers—all with fewer than 150 employees, and representing manufacturing, service, fast food, transportation, construction, and sales sectors. I have also shared my personal perspective as a seasoned employer in my own company for more than eighteen years, with thirty-two staff members in three offices; and as a human resources contractor, consultant, and facilitator. In each of my eighteen years, I noted less than 5 percent voluntary turnover, and throughout the book I share some of the stories that I believe contributed to this low turnover rate. I also 'fess up to many mistakes I made along the way, in the hopes that others can learn from them! The issues of employee retention are extremely complex. I chose the metaphor of sailing (another one of my passions) to hang my learning and writing upon, and I welcome you aboard.

# Introduction

We knew it was coming. First it was a labor shortage crisis, followed soon after by an economic crisis. It's a storm that has been brewing for the past decade, and it has arrived. And it's not going to blow over anytime soon. The situation is clear: there is a lot of work to be done, and in many industries, there are not enough employees available to do it, both in Canada and in the United States. Even amid the current economic downturn, the demographics are working against us as business owners. Baby boomers are leaving the workforce at a faster rate than they can be replaced. Canada has a birth rate of 1.64 children per couple[1] and has not been replacing population since 1970. In the United States, the US Census Bureau indicates that in 2030, one in five Americans are expected to be aged sixty-five or older[2]

In addition, the global competition for talent grows ever fiercer. As companies everywhere brace themselves against this storm, they must look inward to their human resources attitudes and policies, the primary focus of this book. Human resource professionals and economic development researchers believe that employee retention is going to be a key business survival tool, and it is a serious matter. A whopping 81 percent of US executives polled in a 2008 report said that employee retention is an important business priority[3]. But it is not just the loss of talent and experience—employee retention, or lack thereof—that has an enormous impact on your bottom line. Experts tell us that a conservative estimate of the cost of replacing one employee is equal to 1.5 times that employee's annual salary[4]!

Certainly, as a business owner, you might remember the days when you would post an advertisement for a position and then wade your way through piles of résumés, picking and choosing and interviewing among the best of the best. But those golden days are over for the foreseeable future. Businesses everywhere, and particularly small businesses, are already feeling the pinch. The signs—literally and figuratively—are everywhere. And I don't mean just "Help Wanted." Businesses are suffering, even failing entirely, because of a lack of people power! Recently in Victoria, British Columbia, one local pizza joint cancelled Friday night delivery because they could not find a delivery driver. On a Friday night, the busiest night of the week! On a recent trip for a coffee, I was shocked to find my local café was closed at 6:00 AM because the baker had not shown up for work. Another downtown restaurant posted a sign on the door that read: "Due to staffing shortage, we will no longer be open for lunch."

Although the current economic slowdown may provide a temporary reprieve for the labor shortage in some industries, the demographics continue to impact the market, and when the market turns around, your efforts to retain good employees will serve you and your business well.

Unless you've been recognized as a "destination employer" within your industry, those days of prime fishing are probably gone. You might say that in some industries, the labor pool in North America has shrunk to a puddle. Keeping good employees on board will help to ease the pains of the labor crisis, and considering the costs associated with re-hiring and re-training staff, it will also help your bottom line. There is no room to ignore the fact that even in this economy, in many industries, it is still an employees' market and the employees will migrate to employers who fulfill their needs. So what can you do to make your company the one that fulfills those needs? What can you do to be the company that attracts and retains these star employees, ultimately helping your business to succeed and thrive?

The answer: plenty. Employers, managers and supervisors can take advantage of solutions both simple and complex, short term and long term. The benefits to focusing on the issues related to employee retention go beyond affecting the bottom line; in the next two years, they could make or break a company entirely.

Without your employees, you do not have a business—it's as simple as that. And although we keep saying that our employees are our core resource, our most important asset, global research conducted by Towers Perrin 2007–2008 portrays a very different picture. The Towers Perrin Global Workforce Study tapped into the views of 88,000 workers in 18 countries around the world. This unprecedented global research shows that employers may be talking the talk of employee value, but a huge percentage of them are not walking the proverbial walk. In fact, the study showed that only a small fraction, 10 percent, of employees feel they are treated like the most important part of the organization[5].

The issues of employee retention are complex. This book is not meant to provide any type of quick fix. But it will give you, the employer or supervisor, some tools to help you increase your effectiveness in retaining the very best talent. Travel with me, come on aboard as we take a look at what works and what doesn't work, and check out some real case studies of small and medium-sized employers who are excelling at employee retention and reaping the benefits.

# Chapter 1

## Is Your Kit Bag Packed?

*"The pessimist complains about the wind, the optimist expects it to change, and the realist adjusts the sails."* – William Arthur Ward

Employee retention is hard work, and the tools and techniques that will help someone else's team may not be right for yours. This book will help to lead you through the storm with some practical solutions to pressing issues, but you'll need your kit bag. It's not a traditional kit bag, and it's not an easy journey, but the results will be worthwhile. Here are some of the tools, metaphorically speaking, that you will need to adjust your sails during this time of change, to help you successfully navigate through the pitfalls of the volatile labor market.

## A Mirror

There's a reason why this is the first thing on the list. The opportunity to truly look at your own methods, behaviors, biases, beliefs, and attitudes will help you to better understand the relationships that you build with your colleagues, and with the people you supervise. A mirror is a metaphorical learning tool that separates the committed from those who merely hope for external change in order to ensure a smooth voyage. It takes a tremendous amount of courage to pack a mirror. As a manager, a supervisor, a business owner, you have developed your business and all of the success associated with it. As the captain, you are responsible not only for the successful voyages, but also for the groundings and torn sails. Whatever you see around you at your workplace is a reflection of your *own* beliefs, attitudes, and tendencies. How do your surroundings look? Could you do things differently? Are you ready for change? Are some of your behaviors counterproductive to developing and maintaining positive relationships within the company? Sometimes, when you are looking for the problem, you will find it within yourself, and facing this takes a tremendous amount of courage.

As a business owner, I experienced this too many times to recount here, and although being candid with yourself is difficult, the rewards are extraordinary. On one occasion, an employee brought to my attention that when she met with me, I did not pay full attention to her, and was instead glancing back and forth to my computer monitor. Only then did I have that opportunity to look in my mirror and see a distracted, partially engaged listener. It wasn't an easy habit to break, and I eventually learned to turn my monitor off when an employee came to meet with me. This was a small, simple example; I have others that I'll share in the next chapters. The mirror isn't just for the manager or employer, either. It can be presented as a tool for employees. If the owner is willing to model the use of a mirror, it becomes more likely that, with the right supports, an employee will too. The journey is not about who's doing it right or wrong, it's about learning. A mirror is a powerful learning tool. Pack it, and use it wisely.

## A Bungee Cord

"Give 'em an inch and they'll take a mile." That crusty old adage could be slightly changed, and the meaning transformed: "Give 'em an inch and they'll *go* a mile." Employees want and need flexibility. This is especially true for Generation "X" employees, those born between 1965 and 1979 and even more so for Generation "Y"employees, those born after 1980. A bit of flexibility promotes goodwill, and creates opportunities for wins all around. That's not to say that your bungee cord has to strangle the company's operations, or that you need to allow yourself to be held for ransom on your own ship. Guidelines and policies generally rule holiday requests, but keeping a bungee cord packed along for this trip will definitely come in handy. Sometimes, the employees' awareness that you have one aboard can build trust among your employees, and may help you to create your strongest employee retention strategies.

## Sensible Deck Shoes

No serious sailor sets out without a pair of deck shoes. These are not just for "yachties." The treads are specially designed to hold the wearer to the deck, even when the boat is heeled over at angles up to 40 degrees! On a recent sailing trip up the coast of California, we hit some storms that tested my deck shoes as well as my nerve and commitment. I cannot imagine the captain being anywhere else but in the middle of the chaos, leading the way and taking it on the nose. These deck shoes will allow you to be front and center where the action is on your ship, keeping you grounded and steady.

Your very presence, as a strong, dedicated individual, is a valuable employee retention tool. Have you heard the urban business legend of the CEO who changed nothing other than his parking space and witnessed unprecedented growth in the company? The CEO, for years, parked closest to his office door. With the exception of the annual Christmas party, he had little or no contact with his employees. After he changed his parking space to the farthest slot from his desk, he had to walk through every section of the factory before arriving at his office. This simple act allowed him the personal contact that employees craved, and he learned his employees' names, interests, strengths and weaknesses. He also learned about his own. Employee engagement increased and productivity soared. The Towers Perrin research indicates that a *number one* top driver of employee engagement is not wages or benefits or corner offices, but that "senior management is sincerely interested in employee well-being$_2$." You can only do that when you've got on your deck shoes.

## A Bag of Suckers

Pack a small bag of the old fashioned kind, the lolly-on-a-stick kind of sucker. These represent humor. No kit bag is complete without a sense of humor. Have you ever taken yourself too seriously? Who hasn't? A sense of humor can ease the most stressful situations. Just try having a serious meeting, where everyone has a sucker in their mouth. Literally or figuratively, this sense of humor may be your best ally during the voyage. Many companies (Southwest Airlines for example) have used humor as an employee retention tool. It's well known as part of the company culture. Herb Kelleher, founding CEO, has been known to dress up as Elvis, do the chicken dance and infuse humor even into the hiring process to ensure culture fit. Kelleher once told an interviewer that he "couldn't really do anything, so they let me be the CEO. " He told the interviewer how he once arm-wrestled another CEO as way to settle a legal dispute (he won). Kelleher advised managers to "Stop thinking of yourself as professional. Get over yourself and have some fun[3]."

You can't suddenly become funny if it is not in your nature, but if you incorporate humor into everyday events, and allow employees to let their humor blossom, it can embed itself into your culture. Find out where it is bubbling up in your company, and then do everything you can to fan the flames of this value. The story of the small and world-famous Pike Street Market in Seattle is the written authority on fun in the workplace. The book *Fish!* by Stephen Lundin, Harry Paul and John Christensen describes a workplace that is teeming with energy and enthusiasm. This is a real world example of transformation from a seafood counter to a world-renowned destination of customer and employee engagement, entertainment and drama. Play is central in their message. The employees at Pike Street Fish Market know how to play, heaving fish at customers and dealing as much in laughs and entertainment as in seafood. But they don't only play within their team, they include customers. This is not play at the *expense* of work. Instead, play is an integral part of what could otherwise be a tedious job for the employees and an ordinary, forgettable purchase for the customers[4]. When was the last time you had fun buying a fish?

# A Small Trident

Your kit bag is not complete with this celebratory tool. A ceremony is standard procedure on board most ships, large and small, that cross the equator (and many other lines for that matter). Crossing the line. It has been used as an initiation to commemorate a sailor's first crossing of the equator. The story goes that the seasoned sailors initiated the ceremony to be certain that their new crew were capable of handling long and rough seas.

While the celebration has its history of questionable shenanigans not readily transposed into small business culture, it remains, nonetheless, a commemoration worthy of note. After the new crew is initiated, a feast and celebration are enjoyed by all. A celebratory instrument, the trident represents the tool of King Neptune, ruler of the ocean realms.

The trident I used in my consulting business was a thrift store find: a brass bird on a perch. I'm not sure exactly what it was, maybe an eagle or a hawk type of bird. I must confess that it was really quite ugly. It stood about 16 inches high and weighed about 10 pounds. Whenever an employee or supervisor noticed another staff member going above and beyond, or offering help on a project, or initiating something-any type of activity for which one would be thankful-the "eagle" would be presented to that employee at an all-staff meeting. The recipient would have to explain (with the appropriate amount of pride) to clients in the office what the ugly trophy was on his/her desk! There were no rules about how long it would be retained or when the trophy would be passed on to the next person, it just resided as a trident of our culture, a recognition trident that encouraged and rewarded teamwork and excellence. Anything that stands out on a desk could be incorporated and implemented into your organization.

After our arduous trip up the West Coast (did I mention that it was in October?) my husband took me out to dinner and presented me with a medal. A real medal. It is one of those "Victory" medals on a ribbon. On the back he had had engraved "Seamanship: Bravery: Best Friend." With a value of (I'm guessing) 20 bucks, it is nonetheless the most precious gift that I have ever received. It had been a tougher journey than I could have imagined-and I have some extensive offshore miles under my belt. But this simple medal is now a permanent fixture in my handbag, reminding me how far a little recognition goes.

# A Conch Shell

For the purposes of our kit bag, I included the conch shell to represent listening. It's true that you can hear the ocean if you carefully hold the shell to your ear. On board your ship you can also hear the challenges and joys that employees are experiencing by listening carefully. Deep listening is a key employee retention tool, and throughout the chapters, we will concentrate on the importance and the value of deep listening. It is one thing to hear, most people are fortunate to be able to hear, but hearing is not listening. Pack a beautiful and functional conch shell as a reminder to listen as well as to hear.

# A Gourmet Picnic Basket

A part of celebration includes breaking of the bread with crew. Many celebrations centre on the sharing of food, and a well-prepared captain has a store of special delicacies for celebrations large and small. The highest form of inclusion on board a ship is dinner with the captain. This simple tradition is meaningful and represents not only celebration but caring for crew at a basic level. Aboard the Canadian Coast Guard flagship, the *Louis S. St-Laurent*, for example, every Sunday the table is set in the lavish Captain's Dining Room and twelve random crew members are invited to partake in a seven-course gourmet supper. It is a chance for members engaged in very diverse jobs-stewards, scientists, engineers, deckhands-to talk together and enjoy a deluxe meal.

It may be common knowledge that some of the important decisions and ideas are discussed around the water cooler, but this is an idea that is also supported by research. The concept of "open space technology" recognizes that the informal conversations in an organization bear an enormous impact on the organization's cultural norms. The concept of Open Space Technology was created in the mid-1980s by organizational consultant Harrison Owen. He discovered that people attending his conferences loved the coffee breaks better than the formal presentations and plenary sessions and that during the breaks conversations were deep and the participants were highly engaged. He combined that insight with his experience of life in an African village where he observed that village business was conducted around the water well and it was there that important topics were discussed. Owen created a totally new form of conferencing, a meeting methodology that is now widely used all over the world[5].

When the crew really feels that they are included in these informal conversations, when the topic is based on their individual passion, they will provide insights, perspectives, and resources not otherwise available to management. These conversations may or may not include food, but pack a picnic basket into your kitbag and be prepared to break bread to celebrate and learn with the crew and to discover some of the important issues affecting your organization.

## A Small Wooden Plank

You guessed it. A walk-the-plank plank. On any ship, there are times when getting people *off* board is as important as keeping others on board. This book is about keeping good employees on board, but the plank in your kit bag is a reminder that in order to keep good employees on your ship, there may well be some that clearly need to leave. The plank is neither a punishment nor a threat; it is simply one of the important responsibilities of supervisors and managers. In a recent newspaper article about bullying, it was noted that over 60 percent of employers do *not* deal with the bullying that is happening in their organizations[6]. Bullying aside, what is the message to our star employees when inappropriate behavior of any type is ignored and implicitly condoned? For best employee retention strategies, be sure to have this plank packed neatly in your kit bag.

Well there you have it. You're packed and ready to board. You've got:

- A mirror for self reflection

- A bungee cord to keep things flexible

- A bag of suckers for humor

- Sensible deck shoes to keep you where the action is

- A small trident to help mark ceremonies

- A conch shell for deep listening

• A gourmet picnic basket to celebrate with crew

• A small wooden plank for appropriate "off-boarding"

You may want to include countless other items, but these particular tools will prove their worth along the journey. Remember that in a storm, key and essential tools are the ones you need to use most, not flavor-of-the-week strategies. The wisdom of many small and medium-sized employers is contained throughout the next chapters, and you'll recognize the kit-bag tools as they are demonstrated in a variety of examples.

# Chapter 2

## Help New Recruits Get Their Sea legs

*"If you want to build a ship, don't drum up people together to collect wood and don't assign them tasks and work, but rather teach them to long for the endless immensity of the sea"*

– Antoine de Saint-Exupery

Congratulations! You've selected your crew, and they stand ready and waiting to board. In modern human resources lingo, taking on new recruits is called "onboarding!" What happens in the next few days will affect these new recruits for the remainder of their career with your company. In our survey of over five hundred employees, almost a third (32.3 percent) was either dissatisfied or extremely dissatisfied with their initial orientation.

What's a captain to do? Let's start with the usual introductions. A typical orientation in any small to medium sized business usually begins with introducing the new recruit to all of the staff, or at least to the colleagues within their division. It's imperative that the new employee's immediate supervisor is available on this first day. If it's impossible for him/her to be present, arrange for a "welcome aboard" phone call from the supervisor. This creates an initial sense of feeling welcome in the heart and mind of your new recruit. As you conduct your rounds of introductions, pay attention to *how* you introduce each member. You can be assured that this new employee is listening hard for the unspoken messages. Messages with side messages such as: "Don't really pay any attention to George," and "This is Sally, and you'd better not cross her," will make more of an impact than you think. Our tone and mannerisms and choice of words have real opinion-forming power, especially in this early stage for a new employee. Every nuance, every eyebrow raised is noted for future reference. The new recruit is actively trying to get the sense of the culture of your organization. Make introductions as formal or as informal as best represents the culture of your crew. And speaking of the culture, on these first days of employee imprinting, be sure to match the new employee with someone in the organization who represents the most desirable cultural traits that you are trying to nurture. If your new crew spends the day with a disenchanted galley slave, their impression and vision of the company will be tarnished from the start. Better to find a galley slave who cheerfully, or at least willingly, helps with the orientation. Using this type of peer-motivated orientation helps to create an expectation for success right from the outset.

This paying attention to how you describe your organization and the way in which you introduce the rest of the crew is only half of the communication formula. You've completed your selection based on best fit. You have confidence that this new employee has the experience, the cultural "fit," the knowledge and the competencies to do the job- but there is still much to be done in this early orientation stage. Notice your new recruit's comments, observations and questions. These are additional clues for *you*-what excites this person? What more is he disclosing to you about his work values? What can you learn about his interests? In what areas does he need more training? Listen carefully and ask questions as this simple gesture will engage your new employee possibly more than any other act. Pull out that conch shell from your kit bag and do not underestimate the value and the power of listening.

## Tell the Truth!

What? Really. As you introduce the new hire around, tell them about the organization. What matters? Tell them about your proudest moments in the organization. Show off the company awards, the sports trophies, the staffroom plaques. Don't get caught into the trap of telling your new staff what you think they want to hear. If you resort to the team and leadership rhetoric because these are the buzz words, but your organization is *not* team-based or does not promote leadership practices, you will have started off with unrealistic expectations. If you *don't* really invite employee input, don't say that you do. Or, as Brandie Yarish of GenoLogics Inc. so succinctly puts it, "If you don't have beer in your water cooler, don't imply that you do!"

If, however, you are working on a strategy to improve in certain areas, tell them what you're up to. Your honest assessment and evaluation of what's happening in the culture of your organization will pay off in gold in the long term. An orientation is not an event, it is a process. Help your employees by creating an atmosphere of trust. Trust comes (partially) from telling the truth. Starting off with the truth is the best trust-building move you can make. In his book *The Speed of Trust*, Covey's number one recommendation for trust-building is what he calls "Talk Straight." It's more than simply telling the truth, it is "creating a precision of language, an economy of words, and *a lack of spin.*"(emphasis added). This is just one of thirteen behaviors that Covey outlines in developing relationship trust[1].

In the orientation process, you will lay the foundation for a trusting relationship if new crew can expect their supervisor or manager to "talk straight." When new employees came on board, part of our recruitment and orientation included "We are a consulting company, and have been in business for many years. However, our business is contract-based and your position is dependent on the renewal of the contract. I cannot promise to offer you more than one year of employment." You would think that this temporary relationship would limit the degree of engagement on the part of employees. This was not my experience. The employees trusted that I would do everything in my power to grow the business and they trusted the honesty and lack of spin in outlining the temporary nature of any position. Staff consistently and over time delivered exceptional results, many of these staff contributing for over 15 years!

## Safety First!

According to the U.S. Bureau of Labor Statistics, 13 percent of all injuries occur within ninety days of hire, 23 percent occur with the first four hours on the job$_2$! Safety simply cannot wait for tomorrow's agenda. Particularly among youth, the combination of new job exuberance, willingness to perform and lack of experience can literally be a deadly combination. This part of the orientation requires an actual walk around and tour of the entire premises. Safety rules, location of fire escapes, first aid equipment, and hazardous areas can and should be demonstrated, not just provided in a safety manual. Keeping employees safe is the law. Encourage the employee to ask questions, and reinforce the notion that they don't have to know everything right away. This creates an environment where it's OK to make a mistake and most importantly, to ask questions. Never assume that because someone has crewed on another ship, that it's the same on yours. Double check that this new employee has been carefully introduced to each function of her job, and that there is someone assigned to her for questions or clarification.

I was sixteen when I landed my first job as a junior cook at A&W. On my first day, the head cook told me to open the deep fat fryer when the buzzer went off. Then he went out for a coffee break. Being a keener, I tried to open the crank-handle of the fryer immediately, but it was under too much pressure and so despite my best efforts, I wasn't strong enough to open it.

The cook forgot to explain the in-between step...buzzer goes off, *wait* for the pressure to drop on this gauge...*then* open the machine. If I had been strong enough to open it, you can well imagine the disastrous, potentially fatal results.

There are no shortcuts when it comes to safety. Nothing can be overdone on this whole topic. Even after the orientation, safety must be integral to your training program and professional development strategy. Your attention to safety helps new employees to understand your own commitment to this important subject. After the safety tour, provide a checklist with all safety items for the employee to check off that they understand all aspects. A section on safety is included in the Orientation Checklist in chapter tools.

## Right Next to Safety Comes…Celebration!

Celebrate the arrival of this new employee. It's one thing to introduce them around and give a safety overview, but to really connect; you have to celebrate their arrival. You can be sure that if a new person starts off and can't find the washroom, doesn't know anyone's name, and eats lunch alone, that it's going to be pretty much downhill from there. Traditionally, organizations hold a party or celebration when someone leaves the organization. That custom seems a bit backward to me. How about a party when they first arrive? When I was running my consulting practice with 32 staff in three offices, everyone got involved in welcoming new crew. It was truly a celebration. Pizza delivered to the lunch room became standard practice. We used small and inexpensive gestures such as welcome flowers or a banner across their computer to warmly welcome this newcomer into our team. By eating lunch with the whole crew on that first day, a new employee gets the informal cultural cues that are so necessary for survival and engagement in an organization. You can be sure that our new recruits had something to say when they went home and answered the "How was your first day?" barrage of questions from friends and family.

There are some creative examples of organizations that take the new recruit celebrations to heart. Brandie Yarish sends out a welcome aboard package prior to the new employee start date that details where to park, bus routes to the site, and other worksite details to help new recruits prepare for their first day.

## The Big Picture…

Imagine stepping on board a tall ship. It's your first day and you're eager and ready to learn. Your immediate supervisor shows you the ropes-all two hundred and sixty-seven of them. Some of them control the orientation of the sails. Some of them control the angle of the yards to the wind. Some of them collapse the sails, some of them set the sails. To a newcomer, it looks like an incomprehensible mess. Your supervisor then introduces you to your two lines. It's pretty simple, really. Just haul in the two lines that are your responsibility when the ship turns and let them out when the ship is back on course. But wait! What are these lines attached to? How do they work in conjunction with the other lines? Who is steering the ship? Where are we going?

Who takes the lines when I'm not here? What happens if I screw up? What do I do if they get stuck? Does someone tell me when to stop and start? What signs do I look for? Your questions would be countless!

Now, imagine taking this post in a storm, in the dark and without any knowledge of where you're going, or who is at the helm. It's not just that it's dangerous, but without the big picture introduction, you would be at a complete loss as to how to be more efficient, how to anticipate the needs of fellow crewmembers and how to truly operate as a part of a team.

By providing new staff with the big picture, the vision of your organization you are empowering them to make connections within their immediate and not-so-immediate environment which, in turn, results in a deeper understanding of their role. No one operates alone in any business. Our interconnectedness is what makes us productive. Talk to the high-achieving, results-oriented growth companies like Emery Electric. At Emery, they take the big picture seriously. New employees and apprentices are introduced to all aspects of the organization and are provided with a comprehensive safety and orientation training session. Gord Esplen, General Manager at Emery says, "We absolutely care about our employees, as a person, not a number. We hope to develop every single person we take in. And that starts right from the comprehensive orientation. This helps new staff to understand how their work contributes to the company as a whole and ensures that this new recruit has a complete understanding of safety policies."

## Set Goals and Benchmarks-They're MORE Important than Policies and Procedures.

Canadian-owned WestJet Airlines has a recognized culture of fun and flexibility. They also have a pretty simple way of teaching new staff (they're called owners at Westjet, because all employees are shareholders in the company) how to provide the best customer service. Do what you think is right for the customer and we'll back you. They threw out the manual on customer service policies and procedures. Assuming you've hired competent people, then you have to get out of the way, and let them do the job. Westjet wasn't dictating how to treat customers, they gave employees the opportunity to use their best customer service practices without pondering, "am I allowed to do this$_3$?" How many times have you come up against a salesperson who just doesn't know what to do to make a customer happy? "Sorry, sir, I'd like to give you a refund, but I don't think I can." Or, "Yes, ma'am we do have extra bags, but I'm not allowed to give any away." WestJet's unspoken message to their employees is, "I trust that you can make a good decision for the customer and for the company." The expectation is that the customer comes first.

The Tim Horton's example that hit the front page of national newspapers in May 2008, points out the faulty thinking in *not* allowing such employee decision making. "Tim Horton's Employee Fired After Giving Customer's Child a Timbit" read the headline. Ouch! Tim Horton's also retracted the decision and made a hasty public relations move to reinstate the employee immediately. And while this is an extreme example, it may be timely for you to ask yourself: "Could I use benchmarks and goals where I am currently using policies and procedures?" If you want employees to use their own good discretion, you have to hire people who have the ability to make decisions-then you have to *let* them make the decisions.

When people know what is expected of them, and it ties in with the big picture, with the vision of the organization, and they're operating safely… how many policies and procedures do you need? You need some, no argument, and depending on your industry, maybe you need lots. But don't burden a new employee with a 3-inch binder of policies and procedures and then cross your fingers and hope they're going to follow it.

Employees need goals and targets to be able to start on a road of achievement. The "Why are we doing this?" question is often at the forefront of employee motivation. When staff is clear about expectations, only then can they truly perform. The challenge for employers is to find the balance between too much information and not enough. Clear expectations on how to reach company goals and objectives are imperative; extensive directions and rigorous procedures that leave no room for employee judgment are usually too much information.

One of the best ways I know to demonstrate the importance of clear expectations, a simple but imperative concept, was relayed to me by Graham Debling, a professor at Royal Roads University. Debling is a renowned researcher and author in the areas of prior learning assessments. He set up the following demonstration.

Try it with your managers, it takes about 15-20 minutes, and will no doubt be an interesting learning experience.

A group is left in the boardroom-they will become "the audience." Two individuals are taken from the room and each is given a different set of directions. Neither of the two individuals can overhear what the other is being told.

Person "A" is told:

"Your goal is to make the audience laugh and clap. Do or say whatever you like or think will work to make the audience laugh. "

*In this example, Person "A" is not given enough information.*

Person "B" is told:

"Your goal is to make the audience laugh and clap. The only time this will happen is if you use the word "awesome" and you must include lots of body movements. Use your arms in gestures and walk to and fro as you are speaking. They will only laugh and clap if you use these two methods.

*In this example, Person "B" is given some expectations and guidelines for how to meet the objective, without being provided with a 3-ring binder on "How to Make Audiences Laugh."*

Meanwhile, the audience (unbeknown to both of the volunteers who have left the room) has been instructed to laugh and clap *only* if the volunteer uses the word "awesome" and/or integrates lots of body movement into their story or joke.

It's pretty obvious what happens next. One at a time, they come into the room and person "A" has no effect on the audience. Try as he may, with all of his experience at telling jokes - and maybe he's an experienced comedian- he cannot make the audience laugh or clap.

Person "B," regardless of his storytelling ability or memory for good jokes, cannot fail. In response to wild arm gestures and language that is interspersed with "awesome" the audience is clapping and laughing exuberantly.

*Be sure to debrief with both volunteers and audience to ensure that they understand the preparations the audience was given, and also explain that each of the volunteers was given different directions.*

This scenario is indicative of many orientation programs. Some employers or supervisors have systems in place that clearly outline expectations for targets and goals, and *how* to reach them, others miss this important step. Make your company one that provides clear expectations. How else can an employee perform to the best of their ability and produce results that are in alignment with the company's goals?

Remember that orientation is not an event, it's a process. There is real payoff to starting your crew on the right foot. Ask any seasoned sailor and they'll tell you that no one gets their sea legs in a week. And sometimes, when the seas get rough, the sea legs just don't work as well, and so much has to be relearned to get them back. I thought of myself as a seasoned sailor until I reached the 15-foot seas off Cape Mendocino, California. I had to relearn basic survival strategies, some that I had thought were second nature. Survival strategies such as: one rice cake is plenty enough for dinner, and safety harnesses need proper eye hooks for best use!

Provide an orientation that fits the culture of your company and check back with your new recruits on a regular basis to ensure they have had the opportunity to process all of the information.

Orientation is your finest opportunity to reinforce the culture of your organization and to ensure the safety and comfort of your new crew. The orientation checklist in chapter tools may help you to ensure you've covered all of the orientation basics. Now break out that gourmet picnic basket from your kit bag as this is a great time to celebrate with all of crew and especially with your new recruit.

## Chapter Tools

# YOUR COMPANY Inc. *Orientation Checklist*

The following checklist provides a sample that could be modified to suit your particular company structure. It may be completed by the new employee at their own comfortable pace and with the assistance of the peer mentor or supervisor.

Some of the information below is provided prior to the orientation. This checklist is for the employee, to ensure that all of the pertinent information is covered. A follow-up with the new recruit's supervisor may be completed at the end of the first month.

## THE GRAND TOUR    (Supervisor or Peer Mentor - on first day)

_____    Introductions to staff

_____    Tour of entire facilities

_____    Staff room/awards centre

_____    Equipment and machinery

_____    Registration procedures or appointment schedules or ordering systems

_____    Supplies access and supplies requests

_____    Office machines/ IT support systems

_____    Additional special tour add-ons (could include subsidiary office or offsite warehouse or production facility)

## ORGANIZATION   (President, on or before first day)

_____   Our organization and its history

_____   Objectives and philosophy

_____   Our values

_____   Our services

_____   Our clients

_____   Your position


## BENEFITS   (Human Resources Manager, on or before first day)

_____   Special leave days

_____   Professional development

_____   Medical/dental plan

_____   Other


## COMPENSATION   (Human Resources Manager, on or before first day)

_____   Pay rate

_____   Pay schedule

_____   Time sheets or other reporting systems

_____   Overtime

_____   Payroll deductions

_____   Direct deposit options

_____   WorkSafe or insurance plan for employee protection

## LEAVE AND HOLIDAYS    **(Human Resources Manager - usually on first day)**

_____     Holidays/vacation days

_____     Leave policy

_____     Time off requests

_____     Jury Duty

## ATTENDANCE        (Supervisor, on or before first day)

_____     Work hours

_____     Tardiness

_____     Sick/absent days, including expectations for notification

## INTERNAL COMMUNICATION
(Supervisor or Peer Mentor, usually within first week)

_____     Internal communications including meetings, memos and emails

_____     Message slots

_____     Staff room bulletin board

## YOUR COMFORT        (Supervisor or Peer Mentor, on first day)

_____     Coffee and lunch breaks

_____     Bicycle lock-up facilities

_____     Staff room facilities

_____ Smoking policy

_____ Restroom locations

_____ Safeguarding your personal belongings


PERFORMANCE    (Supervisor, usually within first week)

_____ What is expected of you

_____ Performance evaluations schedule and content

_____ Quality

_____ Ethical Standards

_____ Conflict of interest

_____ Probationary period

_____ Dress code

_____ Telephone procedures and courtesy

_____ Promotions

_____ Performance reviews

_____ Discipline process

_____ Causes for terminations

_____ Personal calls and visitors

_____ Suggestions

_____ Equal opportunity

_____ Sexual harassment

_____ Accepting gifts

_____ If you have a problem

## WHAT IS IMPORTANT
(Supervisor or Peer Mentor, within first week)

_____          Values--the four core values of the organization (including examples)

_____          Flexibility

_____          Teamwork

_____          Communication

_____          What we care most about

_____          Other


## TRANSPORTATION          (Supervisor or Peer Mentor, first day)

_____          Reimbursement for travel costs

_____          Parking pass/parking options

_____          Green initiatives, transit options or carpool programs


## HEALTH AND SAFETY (Supervisor or Peer Mentor, first day)

\* Note: The U.S. OSHA is the main federal agency charged with the enforcement of safety and health legislation.

National Occupational Safety and Health board has put together a free safety orientation video and workbook which may be accessed through the following site: http://www.osha-safety-training.net/free.html

In Canada, the Provinces workplace health and safety regulations are administered through WorkSafe (formerly Worker's Compensation Board) and may be accessed by province, for example in British Columbia, see:

http://www.worksafebc.com/

22

Always check with the health and safety regulations pertaining to your industry in your province or state. Keeping workers safe is the law.

At a minimum, start with the basics:

_____ Emergency Procedures

_____ Critical Incidents – Handling and Reporting

_____ In Case of Accident

_____ First Aid

_____ Location of Exits

_____ Location of Fire Extinguishers

_____ Location of Eye Wash Stations


SECURITY (Supervisor or Peer Mentor, within first week)

_____ Security Procedures

_____ Working Alone

_____ Keys

_____ Confidentiality

_____ After Hours Procedures


OTHER

_____ _____

_____ _____

_____ _____

_____ _____

_____  _____

_____  _____

_____  _____

_____  _____

_____  _____

## NOTES

_____

_____

# Chapter 3

## Surefire Ways to Ignite Loyalty

*Leadership is a two-way street, loyalty up and loyalty down. Respect for one's superiors; care for one's crew.* - Grace Murray Hopper

Any captain worth her salt knows that loyalty is a precious commodity aboard a ship. This commodity needs to be actively nurtured, or your crew will be jumping ship faster than you can holler "Man overboard!" There are tools in your kit bag and strategies that can help, not just to ignite loyalty, but to keep it alive. No crew member wakes up thinking, "I don't have any loyalty to this company anymore." They just slowly lose interest and then they disengage from the company, then they leave. In this chapter, we will examine some of the ways loyalty is gained-and lost-along the way.

Your company is where it is today because you understand the keys to *customer* loyalty. Some of the same tools and strategies can be implemented to increase *employee* loyalty. This chapter helps to turn the customer strategies inside-out so that you can use them with employees. And in any labor market, employee loyalty is *as important* as customer loyalty.

## Pride-It's Priceless

One of the most important predecessors for loyalty is pride. Pride in the company and what it represents, pride in the work that is done and pride in the reputation of the company. Let's face it: although "what you do" is not "who you are," work still comprises a large part of the way you define yourself. Employees want to be able to proudly say, "I work for 'X' company." You don't have to be the biggest to be the best. But you do have to know and to crow about what it is that you are good at. ColdStar Freight Systems Inc. is a major player in the freight industry in Western Canada. They helped to develop pride in the company by engaging every single employee in developing the slogan for ColdStar, and the collaborative result was, *"Coldstar Freight Systems, a passionate and respectful company."* This is what the employees noticed about the company, *not* what the CEO declared. The pride in being the trucking company that puts passion and respect into the job has been incorporated into their core values.

Loyalty in the fast-moving "get it there yesterday" freight industry is a core human resources issue. Jennifer Hawes, co- owner and Manager of Human Resources at ColdStar Freight knew after six years of struggling to retain drivers that she must help to develop loyalty or that her company would go under. No better motivator than that. Jennifer told me that there are fifty four thousand truck driver jobs available in Canada at the time of this printing. Without loyalty, they could lose their staff at any job offer that was 25 cents more that what her company paid. Truck drivers, she explained, are a nomadic people resource. The very nature of the job requires them to be on the road, on the go, so finding alternate employment is as simple as "I quit." Well they don't quit at ColdStar. (OK, some do, but the company's retention rates are superb among their industry). What else is ColdStar doing that you can do? Check out the list at the end of this chapter for some considerations that will help your company to ignite more loyalty.

## Vision from the Inside Out

Whether your company is a fast food restaurant or a hotel, whether you provide a service or produce a product, look for the bigger picture of what you're doing for your customers, for your employees, your community, for your world. What is the benefit to any or all of the stakeholders related to your company? Ask your customers. Don't presume to know what it is or why they buy. Just because it's your business doesn't make you the expert on your customers. The simple act of listening to your customers will give you clues to what it is that you're *really selling*. What you are really selling may provide a part of that bigger vision that can be compelling for your employees. At Bean Around the World Coffee, for example, Mike and Maureen are selling far more than just good coffee. People come for the community, the culture, the "scene."

But what if you're selling pizza? Maybe you're freeing up more time for families to spend together? Or maybe providing a break for busy moms? Maybe your ingredients are all local and your business is supporting other small businesses? Maybe your business profits allow you to contribute to a local charity, or a percentage of profits go to a world organization. Maybe you offer staff community volunteer hours or incentives. The possibilities are endless, but every business has the opportunity to provide a vision to its employees that will help those employees to feel some pride in their affiliation with the company.

But it doesn't have to be solely altruistic; maybe the source of pride is all in the making of the best darn pizza in town. Because let's be realistic, most people are in business to make dough, and not the pizza kind! Pride in a superb product translates into pride in the company-and that affects the bottom line positively. This is also an element of branding which marketing executives will tell you is a key competitive advantage. What are you known for? Does it instill pride? James Belasco and Ralph Stayer in their book *Flight of the Buffalo: Soaring to Excellence, Learning to Let Employees Lead* describe the importance of providing vision in order to gain commitment or loyalty. They relate the story of the imaginary executive who takes an employee to a hilltop and points yonder to a luxurious home complete with swimming pool and tennis court. "See that?" the CEO asks.

"Yes," the employee dutifully responds.

"Well," the CEO continues "if you work hard for the next five years, and the company does well—that will all be mine$_1$."

The captain of the ship cannot take lightly the need to create vision that is clear and that fits with employee values, as this will begin to create and nurture loyalty. Company vision needs to be both simple and compelling. A good vision statement helps your crew to understand not only where they are going, but why it matters. A vision is like a snapshot of the future, it's neither a mystical happening nor a bolt of lightning style idea.

Take a look at these vision statement examples:

"Our key is to fulfill dreams through the experiences of motorcycling"

-Harley Davidson

*Note: Who doesn't want to be a part of helping others to fulfill their dreams?*

"Year after year, Westin and its people will be regarded as the best and most sought after hotel and resort management group in North America"

-Westin Hotels

*Note: This includes the people, not just Westin.*

"Whole Foods Market is a dynamic leader in the quality food business. We are a mission-driven company that aims to set the standards of excellence for food retailers. We are building a business in which high standards permeate all aspects of our company. Quality is a state of mind at Whole Foods Market."

-Whole Foods Market

*Note: Employees get to be part of an industry leader that sets the standards. Now that's pride-worthy!*

Countless books and articles are devoted to the topic of vision and a great deal of energy and time are attributed to the development of vision statements. Jim Kouzes and BarryPosner, authors and leadership experts, describe how to "inspire a shared vision" through such practices that could partially be described as cheerleading. Don't fret if you don't see yourself as a cheerleader, as it can be learned, and being inspiring to others includes more than cheerleading, they say. The succinct piece here is to develop a vision that fits for your company, is aligned with your values and is co-created with your key people. Some recommended reading in chapter tools will provide you with some resources regarding vision and how important it is for your company.

## Ignite the Loyalty, and Pass It On

You have much to be proud of. Your company has grown, has developed a reputation within your industry. To ignite loyalty among staff, now it's time to brag. Now is the time to crow from the top of the crows-nest. There are countless awards and examples of this type of business strategy. If we measured the "employee loyalty meter" after such recognition, the change would likely be dramatic.

In October 2000, our youth services team received recognition from a national television station for their creative job search programs. A television crew was sent out to our small office, high ranking ministers attended and the pride was overflowing. The staff had developed and created strategies to assist unemployed youth in the Victoria Capital Regional District. They owned the pride outright and it is still a key point in many of their discussions nearly ten years later. At ColdStar Freight, the awards the company has garnered over the years are proudly displayed in the entrance hall. It's one of the first things a visitor and staff notice as they enter the doorway. At Emery Electric, the employee training certifications are all framed in the main office.

Employees want to be aligned with a company that has a reputation. A good reputation, that is. Any opportunity that employees get to hear or read about the company helps to provide further proof that "their" company is great in others' eyes. And the "their" is acutely imperative. When employees use the language of "my company" and "we" you know that loyalty is alive and well.

At Emery Electric, the source of pride comes largely from their four-generation tradition of excellence in electrical work. It is jokingly referred to as "The Emery Way," and means that new apprentices are taught to do things right. It means more than just avoiding shortcuts, and has everything to do with work ethic and pride being passed down from journeyman to apprentice. The Emery way is to do things right, and their employees are proud of this. At a time when the construction labor pool has nearly evaporated, the long-standing employees' loyalty to the company will keep them on board, and the company comfortably afloat. Derek Emery, owner of the company says "Part of our pride comes from the ongoing training that we offer employees. Keeping everyone current in safety training but also productivity and project management training is a priority. When staff is up-to-date and service levels are up, this instills pride." At Emery, they really do ignite loyalty and they pass it on, just as they have been doing for four generations.

## Blue or Green or In-Between?

We're all familiar with the "green" company. Doing business in an environmentally responsible manner brings about benefits not just for the planet, but for the business. Increasingly, consumers are leaning toward those companies whose environmental practices are clearly benefiting the planet. Likewise, more and more employees are seeking out companies that fit with their environmental values. Your commitment to sustainable and responsible practices is another important element in sustaining employee loyalty. This is especially true for generation "X" (those born between 1965 and 1979) and generation "Y" (those born 1980and later). These employees cut their teeth on the 3 R's of Reduce, Reuse and Recycle - which were very different than the baby boomers' 3 R's. If your company boasts reduction in packaging, organic, local, tree-free products, excellence in recycling, car pool or transit incentives and other eco-friendly practices, you hold a valuable currency for customers and employees.

Here again, you want to crow from the top of the crows-nest your green practices, awards, and commitment to the planet. This is the stuff pride is made of, and again, pride is the foundation of loyalty.

Today, along with the green shift at the forefront of customer and employee consciousness, there is another trend going on, and this one's blue. A blue company is one who has a steadfast commitment to social responsibility and puts their talk into action. There was a time when giving back to the community was viewed as "a nice thing to do." This is no longer the case. Businesses are *expected* to give back to their communities and a growing percentage of customers and employees are scrutinizing the companies who are (and are not) making contributions. Just as in the case of green companies, blue companies are seeing results in their bottom line. Again, it's not all about altruism. There is intense pride on the part of employees who participate in contributing to society as a whole. This may fuel loyalty like no other program or incentive you can implement.

The late Dame Anita Roddick, founder and CEO of The Body Shop developed an environmentally and socially responsible business long before it was fashionable to do so. She set up her first shop in Brighton, England in 1976 and created cruelty-free beauty products that became the benchmark of environmentally sustainable cosmetics. Dame Roddick was a prime example of a business vanguard and an inspiration to many business owners over these past decades. There are so many examples of companies who commit to the greater good of their communities. You don't have to be the biggest ship on the horizon to be able to implement these strategies. Start small, start from the core of your business and slowly build in programs that fit for your community.

Director of Talent and Cultureat Genologics, proudly describes the company's approach to creating socially aware employee events and fundraisers. Each year they organize and participate in the "Canary Derby" for the Canary Foundation, a partner with the BC Cancer Foundation. Employees build and race their home-built cars and last year over $100,000 was raised within the tech community for the cause. It all comes from top management supporting initiatives and suggestions from staff.

"Our CEO totally recognizes that to be a world class organization, we need world class people. World class people are at their best when their day-to-day work has meaning, when they see a greater purpose. Our team is afforded creative flexibility. If our employees suggested an 'Underpants Day' and could demonstrate its value in achieving our vision, it would receive genuine management team support, although I can't guarantee management team participation-that might be pushing it a little but you never know, our Founder did once dye his hair blue." Brandie proudly admitted.

Brandie's key advice:

> *"Know what you stand for, what you value and align your people practices to it - otherwise you get culture by accident."*

Your crew wants and needs to have input into community projects they would like to support. There may be a fine line between genuine enthusiasm for a cause and being "voluntold" to spend your Saturday behind the company banner giving out free doughnuts.

Employees also need opportunities to put forth suggestions, not just opportunities, but also encouragement. Any employer can say "I have an open door policy." Now, what does an open door policy really mean? Formalizing the process may be as simple as a suggestion box, a staff meeting agenda item that encourages suggestions, a newsletter that highlights employee suggestions, or awards that recognize active employee input. An open door policy is *not* an invitation nor encouragement for employees to offer suggestions unless the culture of your organization includes this important feedback mechanism. If crew is afforded the opportunity to offer suggestions, be sure that they have the same opportunity to participate in some way should the suggestion move to the implementation stage.

I once facilitated a workshop in which a company wanted to do some team-building *and* contribute to the community at the same time. They hired the events committee from Platinum Events, Victoria British Columbia, and we created a Build a Bike: Build a Team: Build a Community event. This is a wonderful example of a small scale opportunity to build pride in your team while contributing to the community.[4] In the Platinum example, the teams worked to build bikes from out of a box. They purchased time (by the minute and with Monopoly money) of a volunteering bike shop owner. The bike shop owner then contributed expertise, and tips on how to assemble the mountain bikes. Participants also used the money to rent the various tools to build the bikes. When the afternoon was done, the teams had had an opportunity to experience working in a team, away from the boardroom (and had a lot of fun!) They experienced "team" firsthand and experimented within and outside of their roles at work. But the real learning came, when unbeknownst to the team members, Platinum had connected with the local Big Brothers and Big Sisters organization and in walked two children with their Big Brothers to receive the bikes. The children were delighted; they were unaware that their award recognition was a mountain bike-and the team members were blown away. If there was such a tool as a pride meter, it would have rocketed right off of the scale that afternoon.

## Ambassadors to Keep the Loyalty Flag Flying

Before closing this chapter, there is some value in revisiting the orientation tips. Because loyalty starts at the beginning, remember to use those champions of loyalty for new employee orientation, but also for any media opportunities. Word from an employee's mouth (as opposed to that of the CEO's) often has greater impact because employees may be seen as more impartial toward any particular issue. The ambassadors for your company wear their pride on their sleeves. Find them, recognize them and use their enthusiasm and goodwill to promote your company. This is a particularly important tool in your recruitment strategy, but it also bears well for retention purposes. Fly your flag high and celebrate what you represent. And celebrate those employees who are the key ambassadors for your company.

Loyalty is currency in small business. The opposite of loyalty is mutiny and in the next chapter we'll take a look at ways of avoiding mutiny. Keep your conch shell handy and your ear out of the wind, so that you can listen carefully to what your crew is concerned about—and that is another foundation to both building loyalty and avoiding mutiny.

*"Who can be wise, amazed, temperate and furious,*
*Loyal and neutral in a moment? No man."* -- Shakespeare

# Chapter Tools

Igniting Loyalty Checklist

_____ Do your employees know what the company stands for?

_____ Have you polished your vision statement? Is it clear and compelling?

_____ Have you jointly explored and shared company core values?

_____ Are employees clear about what is rewarded? Do they know the benchmarks or goals that the company is pursuing?

_____ Are employees provided with regular opportunities to give feedback and suggestions?

_____ Does your company post awards, community recognition and media releases in a prominent place?

_____ Is your company involved in social or environmental programs?

_____ Do you know who the loyalty ambassadors are in your company?

Recommended Reading

Vision:

*Guiding Growth: How Vision Keeps Companies on Course,* by Mark Lipton, Harvard Business Press, 2003

Corporate Social Responsibility
For a list of resources/articles on corporate social responsibility, particularly as it pertains to small and medium enterprise, see Vlereck Leuven Gent Management School page of resources at:
http://www.vlerick.com/research/db/search.cfm?menu7=287

see also: Government of Canada / Industry Canada Corporate Social Responsibility: *An Implementation Guide for Canadian Business*
http://www.ic.gc.ca/eic/site/csr-rse.nsf/eng/rs00126.html
and the International Institute for Sustainable Development: *Corporate Social Responsibility and Implementation Guide*
http://www.iisd.org/pdf/2007/csr_guide.pdf        http://www.iisd.org/pdf/2007/csr_guide.pdf:

See also: Odyssey Performance Enhancement Network for philanthropic teambuilding training and tools, Chico California
http://odysseyteams.com/flash-site.php

# Chapter 4

## Avoid Mutiny and Watch Out For Pirates!

*"The ship of democracy that has weathered all storms may sink from the mutiny of those onboard."* – Grover Cleveland

Robert Hendrickson in his book *The Ocean Almanac* regales readers with countless fascinating tales of ruthless pirates and mutineers and stories of bloody battles at sea[1]. Perhaps the most famous naval mutiny tale is the forever popular *Mutiny on the Bounty*. The mutiny against Captain Bligh was due in part to Fletcher Christian's repulsion at the barbaric treatment and torture of his shipmates. Christian and Bligh had developed mutual respect to some degree, so Christian led a bloodless mutiny and set the captain and many of his loyalists out to sea in an open boat. They were not expected to survive, but Bligh's navigation and survival skills proved to be exceptional.

The mutinies of the late centuries occurred because of conditions that could be described as savage or inhumane. Lack of food, terrible living conditions, outright physical torture and abuse, and appalling work conditions all led to dissatisfaction and grumbling in the foc's'le and escalated to many an uprising.

So, times have changed, and although your employees are unlikely to be complaining about maggots in their sea-biscuits, it is important to watch for these warning signs of discontent because it could spell disaster for you and your company. In this chapter, we will explore some of the causes, solutions, and issues around mutiny- and how to successfully defuse a potentially explosive situation.

Although "real" mutiny is far less common than it was in the 19th century, the word itself still holds a great deal of power in our collective psyche. Fast forward a few centuries and we have headlines that include: " Mutiny in the Boardroom"…"The Oxford Rowing Mutiny Revisited"… "Mutiny in the Pews."

From the Bounty to the Boardroom, to the halls of Oxford and into the pews of the church, people anywhere can come together and declare a mutiny. Each of these cases involved an integral frustration and dissatisfaction with the status quo, and in each example, participants felt that their needs were being ignored. Mutiny was, and usually is, a last resort tactic. In any case it is conflict finding its outlet in action. Fortunately, 21st Century mutiny does not involve barbarity or bloodshed, but the results of mass exodus could nonetheless constitute disaster for a small business.

In my example in Chapter 2, where I was working as a cook at A&W (a mere 30 plus years ago), three cooks at the same time gave notice due to the safety issues and general lack of respect that prevailed. I sometimes reflect on the chaos that erupted, not that we couldn't be replaced (there was a ready pool of applicants), but the training and orientation of three new cooks at the same time saw that ship in treacherous waters.

So let's explore conflict in action. It is generally agreed that conflict is good; in fact, healthy corporations and successful small businesses do not avoid conflict. To avoid conflict invites a brewing of sorts, an opportunity for the conflict to grow and fester until participants lose sight of the root cause or it becomes indecipherable. A wise captain will openly discuss areas of conflict, not sweep them away or pretend that they don't exist.

This open and intentional communication is the cornerstone of conflict resolution. As Stephen Covey says, "seek first to understand, then to be understood." In Covey's landmark book, *The Seven Habits of Highly Effective People,* the author outlines how to listen with empathy, to truly change the paradigm of listening.

> "*When I say empathic listening, I mean listening with intent to understand. I mean seeking first to understand, to really understand. It's an entirely different paradigm. Empathic (from empathy) listening gets inside another person's frame of reference. You look through it, you see the world the way they see the world, you understand their paradigm, you understand how they feel$_3$.*"

This is, in practice, far more difficult that it sounds. It is not merely active listening but a practice that involves keen and willing understanding of the person and the issue at stake. Understanding another person's perspective allows you insight into the root of the problem, and a clearer picture of how to help solve the conflict. This communication can only happen through listening with empathy. This is where a captain makes a conscious habit of pulling that conch shell out of the kit bag on a regular basis. Empathic or deep listening takes practice.

In my interview with Captain Greg Sager, owner of Sager's Home Living, he said that a listening device in the kit bag would be the most important tool for a captain. He explained how he listens in order to understand the most important issues his employees may have. "It doesn't always come out the way you think it might," he said, "Sometimes a grievance can be masked in humor, and I have learned to listen very carefully to what staff are saying to get to the heart of what it is they're really telling me." Captain Sager knows the value of being a good listener, and his staff reaps the benefits as well. (They also stay on board). A good rule of thumb for leaders may be to listen more than speak, and to ask questions more often than give answers.

## Peering Through the Johari Window

Communication skills involve more than just listening. When a manager or owner seeks first to understand, he is exploring both the known challenges that prevail and the unknown. A Johari window is a metaphorical tool created by Joseph Luft and Harry Ingham in 1955. Joseph Luft describes the 'Johari Window' in his book *Of Human Interaction* and is dealt with in depth in Luft's *Group Processes: an Introduction to Group Dynamics*.

This classic model is ideal in presenting communication based on levels of self-knowledge and self-disclosure. It is divided into four quadrants and each quadrant represents 'What is known about me'- by myself and by the other person. There are four parts (or "panes," if you will) to the Johari Window:

OPEN: You know and I know.

The open part of communication in this model, describes communications where each person is equal in their level of known information, representing free and open exchange of information.

MASK: You don't know, I know

I may be aware of facts the other person doesn't know. It is my choice whether or when to reveal this mask area information with others.

BLIND: You know, I don't know

The other person may know things about me, of which I am unaware, including habits, or messages that I may unconsciously communicate. This is where the term "my blind spot" is applicable.

POTENTIAL: You don't know, I don't know

Neither party is consciously aware of what is being communicated. Messages that may influence the communication process for good or for bad. This is the area of hidden human potential, where communication can be explored to reveal truths and openness$_4$.

Stephen Covey, in his book *The 7 habits of Highly Effective People* shares the unforgettable story of communication and blind spots in this example of a paradigm shift. A paradigm shift happens when new information provides some type of breakthrough understanding. In his experience, Covey was on a train when a man with his children came aboard. The man sat next to Covey with his eyes closed, oblivious to the noise and rambunctious activity and general disruption that his children were causing. After a while, Covey gently suggested to the man that he try to control his children, that they were disturbing a lot of people. The man turned to Covey and softly replied that he had just come from the hospital where his wife had died an hour ago. The stranger offered that he didn't know what to do, and that the children probably didn't know how to handle it either.[5]

This example highlights how one piece of information changes everything. Beliefs, assumptions, thoughts, feelings, behaviors, all change. A real paradigm shift. Oftentimes when communicating with others there are things you don't know about yourself, or about other people that affects your ability to understand a situation. If you don't know about the levels of unrest or frustration, and if you're not asking questions or exploring the issues, a mutiny could be brewing. Understanding and improving your ability to see yourself as others see you is an enormous leap in favor of good communication skills with your crew. In other words, by pulling the mirror tool out of that kit bag, your awareness of your communication skills will enhance relationships and enable more open and fewer 'blind' communication patterns. Blind spots are often at the root of unresolved conflicts. Unresolved conflicts are the heart of employee dissent and in extreme cases result in mutiny.

## The Five Whys

Another example of how to determine the root cause of conflict is by using what is commonly referred to as "The Five Whys." This technique, used as a problem-solving and communication tool in organizations, was originally developed by Sakichi Toyoda and was later used by the Toyota Motor Corporation. The levels of 'why' help to illuminate the underlying causes of 'symptoms' and can assist in gaining clarity. Here's a sample of asking the right questions to get at the issue:

Conflict Scenario: The chef in a small bistro restaurant is in constant conflict with the line cooks, often resulting in shouting matches, and creating a negative, tense working environment.

**1st Why:**    Why is the chef in conflict with the line cooks?

**A:**   The chef says that he can't keep up with orders and it's the line cooks' fault.

**2nd Why:**   Why is it the line cooks fault that he can't keep up?

**A:**   Because the line cooks regularly call in sick or arrive late – they are unreliable.

**3rd Why:**   Why are the line cooks unreliable?

**A:**   They say they get less than a week's notice of the shift schedule. Some are students and have conflicting schedules.

**4th Why:**   Why don't the line cooks know about their schedules?

**A:**   Because the chef doesn't post shift schedules until Monday of the week being scheduled.

**5th Why:**   Why is the chef posting the schedules so late?

**A:**   Because the chef is also responsible for bi-weekly pay timesheets and must complete these before posting the employee schedules.

This process will not *solve* the conflict but it allows all stakeholders to get a better picture of the chef's frustration and the line cooks' challenges in responding to irregular hours. Prior to applying the Five Whys, major assumptions were based on the symptoms of the discord, creating lots of opportunity for misplaced blame which only served to create more conflict. Restructuring the chef's responsibilities and the timing of scheduling is a solution that a supervisor or owner can tackle far more easily than managing the strife between the chef and line cooks[6].

We all view situations and issues through our unique filters and this aspect of human nature may also provide us with the opportunity to solve problems and conflicts creatively. Two heads are almost always better than one; the trick is to have everyone participate in the process. The captain must encourage good communication that includes honesty and openness, first by modeling it himself.

## Managing the Rumor Mill

Yet another way to avoid mutiny is to manage rumors. Rumors can destroy goodwill, good intentions and good crews if they go unchecked. That age-old game of 'Telephone' where a sentence is whispered from ear to ear, becoming hugely distorted is precisely how rumors are made. On a ship that encourages open communication, where the leaders are trusted and respected, rumors have a more difficult time taking hold. Otherwise, rumors take over and become entrenched as "the truth," creating an environment seething with dissent and mutiny!

During a time of enormous change in my company, we organized a new item for the company newsletter called Rumor Buster. Here, employees were encouraged to post a rumor that they had heard about (without naming sources), and as director, I would respond to the rumor. This actually became a fun activity. It dispelled fears, but at the same time created a vehicle for employees to feel in control of the changes that were developing around them. No second-guessing the "what ifs" as issues of concern became transparent. Tackling rumors before they take hold creates that essential open communication which, in turn, creates trust. Ask your key employees, "What's the latest rumor around here?" You may be shocked to learn what's floating about but the information will guide you to managing the proverbial rumor mill. And again, it may be rather fun.

## Leading Change to Avoid Mutiny

You will notice that I called this *leading* change not *managing* change. You can manage the rumor mill, as in the last section; but you must lead change. Applying good leadership to change gives your crew the vision and the reasons to follow that vision. During times of change in a company, especially a small business, the stress of the unknown can grow into a full scale mutiny. As a captain on a small ship, the responsibility of managing transitions and change can be overwhelming. Communication, again, is vital.

I was invited to deliver a series of workshops on organizational change. A large health services company was making some changes to their district and regional model which would, among other things, change reporting structures for many employees. I had lengthy meetings with senior management to determine the effects of the change, and the current levels of employee understanding. On the morning of the workshop, I introduced some change models, and various ways of managing transitions. It became evidently clear to me that the employees had NO idea of what the change was that I was speaking of! I called an early coffee break and spoke to senior management (who were in attendance) about my serious concern for the participants. "Oh no, they have been told," I was informed. I insisted that senior management address the staff in the workshop. The CEO came back after coffee and addressed the group. He apologized for the lack of communication. He clearly outlined the new reporting model, and he assured employees that there would be no job losses. The employees were now ready to explore ways of moving ahead with the changes.

A captain must never, never assume that people know what is going on. Clear and repetitive messages are imperative during times of change to ensure the safety (the emotional safety) of the crew.

In my own business, we were going through some of our own organizational changes. Our primary work had been related to career and employment consulting and we were branching out to integrate more corporate and business consulting. One way to ensure that staff was really on board with the changes involved some experiential learning--the *learning by doing* methodology, not just listening to information about change.

In an article I wrote for the BC Human Resources Managers Association, I outlined one way of incorporating experiential learning into the workplace as a way of leading change. Here's the article: (reprinted with permission)

"We know that strong teams are integral to high performance organizations. Maybe it really is time to get out of the 'bored' room with staff. Experiential learning is learning by doing. It happens as a process when individuals engage in some activity, reflect upon that experience or activity and gain some useful analysis. The result is the application of that learning through a change of understanding or behavior. Effective experiential learning will affect the learner's cognitive structures and attitudes, perceptions and behavioral patterns. As an example, take that last meeting you attended and view it as a learning scenario. Were people engaged? Was the meeting productive? Did participants gain new insights or did the meeting serve to reinforce learned behaviors that may have been counter-productive to achieving results?

Experiential learning creates an environment that can be fun; it encourages risk taking-- particularly risk taking within the arena of experimentation with various roles. As participants gain insights into their own and others' communication styles, roles and group interactions, they have the opportunity to experiment and challenge their beliefs about 'the ways things are' in their organization. The opportunity to work together outside of the context of work, but with a common goal as the task, opens the door to meaningful dialogue. For instance, as the team develops generative metaphors, the learning creates a "language" that may become part of the "common language" in the organization. The common language can become a springboard for new approaches to old problems.

Let me share with you an example from my own team. We were undergoing some major changes. With 32 staff at the time, we could have had meetings to discuss the changes, but what was important was increasing each individual's capacity to change. Instead of meetings, we created a treasure map that was divided between three offices.
All three offices had to work together to determine:

- The meeting site (it was a park forest on the outskirts of the city)

- Individual responsibilities, some for setting the course, others for arranging coffee and refreshments in a hilltop setting.


When all was said and especially *done,* all staff was not only knowledgeable about the changes, they were a part of them. They had had to change their routine of coming into work, of reporting structures and were afforded the opportunity for real input into the new model of doing business.

At the end of the day, following an afternoon adventure program low ropes course and a tremendous amount of fun, the feedback was exceptionally positive. Change didn't seem so frightening, and the new common language that developed throughout the day led to a new form of dialogue for expressing concerns and ideas. Staff had had an opportunity to 'experience change'; a real departure from 'talking about change'. We literally walked the talk of change.

Maybe it really is time to get out of the "bored" room. Experiment. Learn! And most importantly…have *fun!*"

The exercise that staff completed following the experiential learning is included in Chapter Tools.

Asking questions helps to point employees in the direction of understanding changes that affect them, understanding at a deeper level so that they can better cope. There cannot be too much information shared with staff when they are in the midst of change. And memos alone just don't feed most employees hunger for information

So, Captain…avoiding mutiny inevitably involves communication, communication and communication. Do not assume that your crew has enough information about what's going on aboard your ship. Develop systems and strategies that will help to keep dialogue open, even during a storm. A treasure chest of tools and samples are included in Chapter Tools.

## Watch out for Pirates!

Mutiny is the furthest thought on your mind. Your talented crew is content, you're sailing along nicely and the sea is calm. But what is that ahead? Another ship is fast approaching and armed to the gunnels with modern day headhunters, poachers, and pirates-and they're coming to get your crew!

As Brandie Yarish at Genologics said, "there's probably not one of our staff who hasn't been approached by another company." The savvy Genologics CEO knows that in building a world class organization, they needed world class people to run the company. The challenge with running a company with talented people is that the competition wants them too. In times of labor shortage, the demand outweighs the supply and every company is vulnerable.

"But they don't leave do they?" I continued the conversation with Brandie.

"No. In most cases they do not." Brandie responded.

So what is Genologics doing to keep them-even when crew is being offered an extra ration of grog by the pirates? Brandie described an extensive and foundational approach they took in developing their human resources plan. First of all, they rebranded human resources. You see, Brandie is not the Human Resources manager. She is the Director of Talent and Culture. How impressive is that? But the work is not about fancy titles and semantics. A foundational road map was developed that was a full year in the making. It's one of Brandie's proudest achievements. The foundational road map was primarily based on values. Corporate values were well-defined and clear and compelling. Brandie explained that once the shared values were in place, everything else was built around those values.

Here's a way of exploring values…what do you suppose is the most stressful job in the world? Air traffic controller? Police officer? Hostage negotiator? It isn't the nature of the work that makes a job stressful-it is the misalignment of individual values versus organizational values. If one's values are misaligned with the work they do, if someone has to park their values at the door to go to work, the stress is beyond measure. At Genologics, Brandie makes certain there is a values match, an alignment between new recruits and those of the organization. This clear alignment helps the talented crew to continue to develop commitment to their work place, which in turn, makes it difficult for poachers or pirates to lure them away.

Values are reflected in your actions, in the areas that you speak about, pay attention to, promote to others, spend your money on and are proud of. Many organizations spout values that have extremely dubious and questionable origins. Not surprisingly, one of the most common is teamwork, but saying something or writing it down does not magically make it part of your values system. If you prefer to work alone, reward individual achievement, and prefer to lead than follow, it doesn't make sense to print "ALL ABOUT TEAMWORK!" on your company's sign.

Recently, I was standing in line in my bank, when I noticed a large, beautifully designed poster proclaiming the company's values. Ever curious about such things, I asked the young service representative how the bank came up with those values. "I don't know" he politely replied, "I think head office made them up." Values are not words on a wall or a company poster, they are what the company demonstrates day in and day out.

One of my values is humor. It was developed and agreed upon as a corporate value by all members of the staff at our annual company retreat in the early years of my business. One day my sister came to my office to meet me for lunch. She waited in the reception area for a few minutes while I finished a telephone call. When we were leaving the building she said "Your office is so noisy. I couldn't work in an office that's that noisy. I could hear people laughing all the way down the hall." My sister worked in an accounting office, and you can imagine how inappropriate it might be for accountants to be laughing when a client arrived to pick up year end statements! But in our office, we are in the people business. Many of our regular clients joined in the fun, and I was told on many occasions that we provided a model of a positive work environment (this often from unemployed clients, some of whom had only negative images of what work could be.) Humor was entrenched and infused into our culture. That noisy, rambunctious laughter is what I miss most since my transition to becoming a solo consultant.

Clear values established in the workplace provide good insurance against the poachers. People don't just want jobs. Their lives are more about values in action. Staff seek to fulfill mental and social and spiritual needs, and if the workplace is in alignment with these needs and values, your retention rates will prove positive over and over again. Remember in Chapter 3, the idea that even if you're serving pizza, key values are in play. Your staff may value family and working as part of team that creates family meals. In an organization that appreciates family time and makes allowances for staff to attend to family matters, you are making active that value most important to that employee.

Sometimes, however, even with all the right tools on board, with engaged employees who are living their values, you can still lose crew members to pirates. I attended a workshop in Regina, Saskatchewan in February, 2008- led by Peggie Koenig, Principal of Koenig and Associates Inc., the largest private Human Resources company in Saskatchewan. Peggie was teaching employee retention strategies in this particular workshop. She began the session by relating that just one hour before her presentation she had received an email on her Blackberry that one of her "star" employees was leaving. This employee had been poached by a competitor, and Peggie was very much concerned about how she would replace this gap in talent. What incredible courage. What a wonderful model of leadership, of living what you teach, and modeling the humility and beauty of being human in a human resources field. She shared this real life example, and I learned lessons from Peggie in that workshop that were not on the agenda$_8$. Even when all the best tools and strategies and care and concern are in place, sometimes, companies just cannot compete with the poachers. Letting go of talent can be difficult, but at the same time, when you really do care for your crew, it's important to recognize that this may be the best move for that particular crew member.

The pirates are out there. Develop your strategies that will help to keep valued talent and seasoned sailors on board. Be sure to double check that you are clear about your values, and understand the values of your crew. Listen carefully and understand what your employees want and why they stay. These actions are protection against the pirates, but at the end of the day there is no magic that can keep your crew with you, so humbly let that star employee go and know that this is likely the best thing for them to do. As for you? Why do you think Captains keep a stash of rum?

# Chapter Tools

## Key Reminders for Avoiding Mutiny

_____ Do you have systems in place that formalize communications?

_____ A newsletter?

_____Easy access to supervisor/manager/ CEO?

_____Do you have clear procedures on how to bring forward concerns?

_____Is conflict in the open?

_____ Do you know what your crew's current concerns are?

_____Are you clear about your values?

_____Do you know what is most important to each of your staff?

_____Do you know what the rumors are on board your ship?

_____Are rumors managed before they get entrenched as the truth?

_____If your organization in the throes of major changes-Are you communicating regularly and repeatedly to ensure understanding?

_____Are you telling the truth about the changes? (i.e. no spins or glossing over possible negative effects?

_____Is there a compelling reason to change?

_____Do staff know what the reason is for the change?

_____Are timelines and reporting structures outlined in the change stragegy?

_____Do you know your crew's concerns related to the change strategies?

_____Does each crew member know how the change will affect them? This next section is the document that I used for the above experiential learning day in the forest.

## Walking the Talk of Change

This is the exercise that I used following our experiential learning day. You can modify it to fit any change your business is undergoing, but the basic premise is still about communicating the change effectively, and encouraging participation and openness in the process.

Debriefing the First Part of the Day
Think about what you had to do *differently* to get to work today. What kinds of changes did you experience? List some of them below:

- Go back even further to the problem solving process of your particular office, and observations you may have had regarding other offices' processes? Think about how you determined the location for this meeting?

- Who determined how the exercise would be conducted?

- Where did the faxing the three offices' puzzle pieces idea originate?

- What was it like to piece a puzzle together without "the cover picture"?

- What was your role in the exercise?

- Was this role typical or atypical for you?

- What assumptions did you make?

- How did you determine what were assumptions and what were truths?

- Would you describe your actions as pro-active or reactive?

Think about your reactions to the changes. They may range from frustration to exhilaration and maybe everything in between. ALL of these are normal reactions to change. None are right or wrong. Often the reactions may swing from one extreme to another within a very short time frame. There is, however, value and meaning as you explore your reactions to change. Ask yourself questions such as:

- Did I expect this reaction or was I blind-sided by it?

- What other stressors in my life may have impacted on my reactions to change?

- How do I typically react to change?

- What do I need to prepare for change?

- Did I gather enough information from the day about our changes?

- Some things that are still unclear for me include:

- Who can I ask for help with this?

- Who can I lean on and especially, who can I get answers from?

- What are my three main concerns at this time?

Review these questions, make adjustments by adding new examples or deleting some that just don't apply to your unique situation. The most succinct part is the understanding why and how your crew is coping when you're in the midst of a course change. Don't underestimate the incredible power of communication at all levels during these times of change.

## Recommended Readings About Change:

*Managing Transitions: Making the Most of Change* by William Bridges Persueus Books New York, NY 1991

*Leading Change: The Argument for Values Based Leadership* by: James O'Toole Random House Publishing, Toronto, Canada, 1996 Originally published by Jossey Bass USA ,1995

# Chapter 5

## Different Strokes for Different Folks

*"What is tolerance? It is the consequence of humanity. We are all formed of frailty and error; let us pardon reciprocally each other's folly-that is the first law of nature."* - Voltaire

Today's workforce, more than ever before, is made up of people from drastically varying social, generational, geographical, and cultural backgrounds. Additionally, in a time where it is not only acceptable but *expected* that a worker will change careers up to five times in their life, you may encounter any level of competency and knowledge at any age. Whoa! What a mixed-up recipe for a disastrous voyage, you might be tempted to think, as the captain of this new and very different ship. But, with a little bit of tolerance and willingness to adapt and change, you will find that the rewards of incorporating the unique skills and attitudes of these different viewpoints are better than the richest treasure spoils of Tortola.

This section comes with only one introductory apology. I am not pigeonholing or stereotyping groups of people. So to those who take any offense, please pardon my "frailty and error" and I assure you that no offense is intended. That said, it is imperative to have some understanding of the basic differences in work values and characteristics whether they be generational differences, cultural differences, individual characteristics, or competency-based discrepancies. Whatever the source, it requires you, as captain, to adapt to these differences and to really use that conch shell you packed into your kit bag. And maybe a few of those suckers too.

## Different Strokes for Different Generations

At any time you may have up to four different generations working together aboard your ship, so you will want to gain a greater understanding of the differences which are partly rooted in the generational divides. You've heard of Generation X (those born between 1965–1979); Generation Y (those born between 1980-1999); The "Traditionalists" (born between 1922-1945) and of course, the "Boomers"(1946-1964)[1.] It is true that each group brings different gifts and different challenges to the workplace. They also share lots of common ground such as preferring a workplace that is respectful and where their work is valued. A better understanding of these groups will help you to gain clarity and develop tools to help you to communicate effectively and to create the best environment to motivate your crew.

In this section we'll explore the four generations that make up the workplace and discover the work environment that each generation prefers. We'll also explore the communication styles of each generation and identify strategies for effective communication on board your ship.

There has been much research and dialogue about the generations and their work ethics and work values. The prevailing ideology is that values are a major driving force in work satisfaction, and that each of the generations described has distinctly different values. It's important to understand that each generation has developed some values that correspond with their generational group. These values are partly based on the events that shaped their upbringing and are often reflected in the behaviors that shape their work ethic.

Let's start by looking at the *core values* of these groups, and some of the influencing and defining events that shape their work ethics as a whole:

Our "Traditionalists," (I'll call them the "Old Salts") come on board the ship with years of experience and with lots of sea miles under their belts. They have respect for authority and a clearly defined sense of right and wrong. Honor may well be their operative word. Our Old Salts have experienced the Great Depression and WWII among other major life-altering events. No surprise that they are loyal, that they stay with a company. They grew up when changing jobs was not an option, and authority was everything. This group prefers hierarchal organizational structure and favors straightforward and logical communication.

Next to step aboard are the "Boomers." From here on-in I'll refer to them as the "Seasoned Sailors." The Seasoned Sailors have a solid, strong work ethic, value personal gratification and involvement, and operate best as team players. Seasoned Sailors have different, but equally defining events that have shaped their characteristics and core values. Seasoned sailors came from an era of social unrest and one where music and the prevalence of "freedom"was unveiling itself nightly on their new TV's. They also experienced the effects of the Cold War. The Seasoned Sailors are often the workaholics -work first, everything else second-but they want personal satisfaction in their careers. In fact, they want it all.

Make way now for Generation X whom I've dubbed "Neptune's Children." This generation values diversity, self-reliance and flexibility. Neptune's Children were influenced by Sesame Street, Game Boy, and a divorce rate that tripled over previous generations. This is the generation for whom the phrase "latch key children" was coined. No surprise then, that this group favors work environments that encourage self reliance and the opportunity to build a portable career. Neptune's Children question the relevance and authority of many institutions and are highly adaptive to change and technology.

Now, for the up-and-coming Generation Y, "The Greenhorns" whose core values include diversity and success, and whose defining phrase may well be "anything is possible." Technology exploded just as they were coming into the world, and through the use of technology, extremely violent events unfolded before their eyes. They have been witness to countless natural and manmade disasters. This is also the empowered generation of "family meetings" and equality, where everyone on the baseball team gets the trophy and there's no such thing as an MVP. Communication with Generation 'Y' needs to include the answer to their ever-questioning "Why?"

This short review of the generations and some of the defining events of each may help to shape the paradigm from which you may view the diverse groups in your crew. So how can you use this information and awareness about the differences existing on your ship? Sometimes just bringing about that awareness of differences in of communication styles and values can break down barriers. You may be thinking, "No wonder my 19-year-old employee is such a great multi-tasker and loves all the new electronic navigation tools. Also, no wonder that his sense of entitlement kicks in regularly, as he expects to be captain, though he only started last week!"

It may help to explain why the "Old Salt" is loyal to the authority and to the organization and the "Greenhorns," meanwhile are loyal to people, and to causes, not to organizations.

Here are some key suggestions you may consider for each group:

*For All Groups:*

Double-check that your respect factors and good listening skills are well honed. Though they may be different, all workers want to know how their work affects the whole organization, and how their part contributes to the whole. Provide development opportunities for all staff by meeting them where they are, and helping them to get to where they can best contribute also remember to recognize this progress along the way. Wherever and however possible, coach your star sailors whether they are 17 or 72. (More on coaching next chapter)

*For Old Salts:*

Acknowledge special effort and preferably provide public acknowledgement.

Explain reasons behind decisions, especially decisions affecting this employee.

Clearly communicate reporting channels/methods.

*For Seasoned Sailors:*
Highlight life and work balance needs and provide opportunities to implement same.
Discuss their personal and career goals.
Provide feedback that is well documented.

*For Neptune's Children:*
Offer a flexible work environment.
Create opportunities for, and reward, initiative.
Do *not* micro-manage.

*For Greenhorns:*
Tell them the "Why," not just the "How."
Create personalized work environments.
Provide them with challenging assignments.

Ginger Brunner is president at Dynamic HR Solutions Inc., a Canadian Human Resources company that has trained hundreds of different types of organizations how to bridge generation gaps at work. Ginger's personal story of being the youngest member on the executive team at a major hotel highlights some of the things she learned about the generational divide. In this situation, Ginger had regular and frequent contact with a lateral manager. Over a short period of time, she noted this manager's lack of response and increasing lack of communication and support on cooperative initiatives. As a typical Neptune's Child, Ginger had primarily been using email as a communications medium. When she sought more understanding about the rift that was developing, the Old Salt manager explained that he doesn't like email, doesn't have time for it and typically put emails into a folder for later viewing. When "later" became never, he didn't realize that anyone had noticed. After some friendly discussion, Ginger changed her main method of communication with this manager. This may also represent a small paradigm shift. Through open communication, she mitigated some potential conflict before the conflict had time to really take hold. And Ginger got clarification on what she was doing right and what she could do differently-that essential feedback that Neptune's Children crave. One could argue that the example above is not a generational conflict, but a communication or technological conflict. Because loyalty and other values are steeped in experiences often unrelated to unfolding events, these generational snapshots help to give some context to an extremely complex subject.

Any captain can seek to understand differences and may display the willingness to consider generational differences. To do this well, it is advisable to make it clear that you see the person in front of you as an individual, as well as a part of a generational group- to create an environment that promotes tolerance. As in the development of any characteristic that you wish for your employees, the first step is to first demonstrate and model tolerance yourself. For all crew, regardless of generation, what you *do* is what others notice, *not* what you say.

The chart in the chapter tools is from Dynamic HR Solutions Inc. It provides a quick matrix of the generations and the environments and communication styles that fit each.

## Different Strokes for Different Attitude Approaches

How you view your employees, regardless of their generational background, will greatly influence employee retention. In this section, we depart from the Generation 'X' and Generation 'Y' concepts and explore a whole new way of viewing an employer's attitudinal differences that affect employee motivation. Theory 'X' and Theory 'Y' refers to the seminal work of Douglas McGregor.

McGregor submits that in a typical hierarchal organization, work is based upon certain assumptions about human nature and human motivation. Those basic assumptions about people and why they work can be divided into two categories: Theory 'X' and Theory 'Y'. Theory 'X' assumes that most people prefer to be directed, are not interested in assuming responsibility and above all, want safety. Managers who accept this theory may view their staff as unreliable and irresponsible, and attempt to control every aspect of the work, closely supervising their charges. McGregor concluded that Theory 'X', when broadly applied, may indeed fail to motivate many individuals to work toward the organization's goals.

In contrast, or as an alternate theory of human behavior, McGregor detailed Theory 'Y' as an attitude that people are not, by nature, lazy and unreliable. He posits that people can be self-directed, that work can be as natural as play if the conditions are favorable.

These theories are described in Paul Hershey and Kenneth Blanchard's Sixth Edition of *Management of Organizational Behavior*:

> "Theory X and Theory Y are attitudes, or predispositions, toward people. Thus although the best assumptions for a manager to have may be Theory Y, it may not be appropriate to behave consistently with those assumptions all the time. Managers may have Theory Y assumptions about human nature, but they may find it necessary to behave in a very directive, controlling manner…with some people in the short run to help them "grow up until they are truly Theory Y acting people $_2$."

From an academic review to the real-life experience of a practitioner operating a successful coffee shop: Maureen Gardin of Bean Around the World. Maureen describes how she and her husband, Mike view their staff:

> "I think an employer has two attitudes that they can choose… the first is:
> I am lucky to have these employees. Without these staff, my business wouldn't exist.
> The second attitude choice is:
> These employees are lucky to have a job, and they'd better darned well do as I say. I subscribe to the first way of thinking and approaching my staff. If they're ready to take on new challenges, I give them every opportunity to succeed."

That's Maureen's version of Theory 'X' and Theory 'Y'. If you stop by "Bean Around the World" you'll see happy employees - and they stay on board! I talked to one of the coffee wizards, Zach North, who had been employed at the little coffee shop for almost three years. He told me that he's been working with most of the same crew for over two years. "What makes you stay?" I asked.

"Mike and Maureen are available and they listen. They care for the employees, and it's a lot of fun. We like coming to work, it's respect. I work very hard and it doesn't go unnoticed."

If your crew doesn't sound at all like Zach North, ask yourself, "What is my prevailing attitude toward employees?" And, more importantly, be willing to listen to your own answer!

## Different Strokes for Different Levels of Crew Readiness

Countless theories, discussions and books detail a myriad of human behavior theories which we don't even touch on here, but one more concept that we cannot overlook is referred to as "situational leadership" and it's worth looking at for any work situation regardless of the demographics of your crew.

Kenneth Blanchard and Paul Hersey have developed this model of leadership theory which, stated most briefly suggests that "the behaviors used by managers or supervisors are most effective when directly related to the *readiness* of the learner. The task at hand and the relationship between manager and learner must be balanced. Coupled with the learner's readiness or competence is the learner's commitment.

The Follower (or usually crew) scale ranges from:

**Low Competence, Low Commitment**: fairly new on board, has some previous experience, somewhat hesitant to learn or take direction. Hershey/Blanchard categorize this as **R1,** Readiness Level 1: Unable and insecure or unwilling

**Low Competence, High Commitment**: someone new on board, eager to learn, but has never handled a sail. Hershey/Blanchard categorize this as **R2,** Unable but Confident or Willing

**High Competence, Variable Commitment**: Seasoned crew, maybe has not done this particular task before without help, may not be motivated to complete task well or quickly. Hershey/Blanchard categorize this as **R3,** Able but Insecure or Unwilling

**High Competence, High Commitment**: this crew has been on the team long enough to be highly competent and confident in their ability, fully committed. Hershey/Blanchard categorize this as: **R4,** Able and Confident and Willing

Even these developmental levels are situational. A senior officer on a ship may be High Competence and High Commitment until he must address a situation that he is uncomfortable addressing, i.e. asking someone to walk the plank.

Next comes the matching of the leader's style to the follower's level of development. In order to successfully apply situational leadership, a leader must be aware of style and cognizant of the current readiness level of the follower. The task behavior could be described as the Who/What/When. Directing-controlling type behaviors and the relationship behavior fit more into the realm of supporting, communicating, facilitating, and providing feedback.

The Manager's (or Leader's) scale of behavior looks something like this:

**S1: At the "telling" stage** the leader is directing, supervising, providing specific instructions.

**S2: At  the "selling" stage** the leader is explaining decisions and providing opportunity for clarification

**S3: At the "participating" stage** the leader is participating, encouraging, collaborating

**S4: At the "delegating" stage** the leader is delegating, observing, monitoring, fulfilling.

A goal in understanding this leader-follower situational model may be to observe how you currently and predominantly lead your crew. If it's primarily at Level 1 (telling, directing, controlling) and your crew are experienced (and likely frustrated) you may need to review alternate behaviors to encourage their development to a more productive level. No employee develops in a climate of "I know you already know this, but let me show you how it's really done."

Likewise, if you typically operate at the delegating stage, but crew are new and lacking in confidence, the mismatch may cause crew to feel incompetent, when all they needed was more telling or selling to get them on their way. Then you could utilize a delegating style once crew demonstrated that higher level of readiness. It's wise to pay attention to the level of readiness each employee demonstrates. Take the time to understand crew *ability* and *willingness*. Ideally, this will drive a supervisor's behavior toward individual needs.

Hershey/Blanchard's model of situational leadership is well worth further exploration as we have only scratched the surface here$_3$. The important element to remember is that each crew brings different readiness levels, competencies, and motivation to the ship and a wise captain will adjust her style accordingly.

## Different Strokes for Different Cultures

Lastly, it's important to look at cultural differences in valuing diversity in the workplace. Christine Stoneman, a principal of Chemistry Consulting Group shines the light on the need for immigration as an important strategy in a labor supply crisis. "Overall there has got to be more immigration to keep the engine running." In 2007 Stoneman began working with the hospitality industry in Canada to help build a bridge between employer needs and foreign workers. She conducts workshops in the Philippines to help screen and interview potential candidates for jobs in British Columbia, Canada and to help new workers to prepare for potential culture shock$_4$. Alison Peever works with Christine as a foreign worker specialist. According to Peever, the foreign workers are the ones who are "making it happen in our economy." Alison knows the unique needs of foreign workers and works with employers to help them create satisfying employment and career opportunities for the benefit of both parties. Alison suggests that employers who understand at the outset that language difficulties can be overcome, and that a little empathy goes a long way will be successful in tapping into this highly committed and hard working labor pool. She gave examples of employers providing whale-watching opportunities or tickets to hockey games as ways of helping foreign workers feel connected to their new communities.

Chemistry Consulting Group knows what they're teaching others... they walk the talk of workplace excellence. Chemistry Consulting Group Inc. ranked second in the Best Companies to Work For- Companies with fewer than 100 employees-by BC Business Magazine, 2008.

Foreign workers need supports and understanding of their cultural background in order to successfully integrate into the North American labor market. Employers can do much to create a work atmosphere that supports a diverse work force. One way to demonstrate respect is to show a genuine interest in the culture of your employees.

Viet Tran is the Program Director of the Employment Transitions and Coaching Program at Victoria's Immigrant and Refugee Centre Society. Tran's extensive knowledge and experience in helping employers to adjust to a multicultural workforce translates into one key recommendation that he offers employers:

> *"Don't make assumptions. Learn what certain behaviors or characteristics of different cultures mean. This is important for the retention of multi-cultural workers."*

Too often, assumptions are based on our own world view. An example Tran offered was his experience in coaching an employer who had taken on a new worker whose English-speaking skills were minimal. The employer phoned Tran to explain that this worker "really didn't want to work"…that he (employer) would give him instructions and the new crew would indicate "yes, yes" and then *not* do as he had been instructed. Tran suggested that the employer ask the employee to repeat back what he understood needed to be done. The employee wanted to work, was motivated to work, but clearly, it turned out, could not understand the directions he had been given. The employer took the time to implement Tran's suggestion and soon called back to say, "I forgot. I was a new Canadian myself at one time, and still I forgot how difficult it is to be given instructions in a foreign language." The simple remedy was to have the new crew repeat back or demonstrate his understanding of the instructions.

In our chapter tools Victoria Immigrant and Refugee Centre Society has provided a checklist of tips to help retain productive people.

My own experiences in supporting diversity includes the time we welcomed aboard a talented and hard working single mom, a member of the Sikh faith. On one occasion, her father was hosting a week long feast at the Sikh Temple. Staff and supervisors alike joined this member of our team at her temple for the celebration feast. Staff was afforded an extra-long paid lunch break in order to participate. This experience allowed all staff to gain appreciation and increased understanding of this culture and it brought our Sikh staff member increased respect and support from all crew. Small remembrances and appreciation for unique circumstances don't cost a lot of money. They indicate a genuine concern for individuality and go a long way toward promoting that all-important loyalty.

Other examples, not tied to diversity, but certainly in support of individuals included a "wedding dress tour"; staff at one of our offices walked a few blocks to a showing of our manager's wedding dress. It was quite a sight…all the male and female staff marching down the street, then sitting in the rows of chairs while their manager tried on her wedding dress and came out to model it for everyone.

Another similar example: a young office worker had just bought her first new home. We all piled into two vans and did a quick drive-by inspection of her new digs. These are such small gestures to support the interests of staff. Different strokes for different folks, but it worked for us.

And what do employees in our own survey say about their employers' valuing diversity in the workplace? Good news. Over 50 percent of the over five hundred employees surveyed indicated that they were either very satisfied or extremely satisfied that a culture of individuality was respected in the workplace.

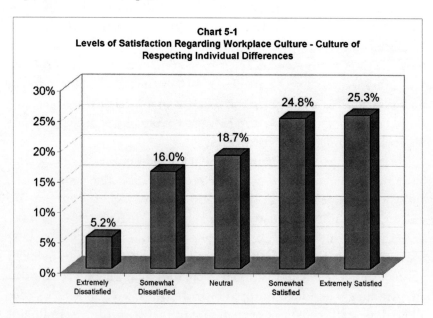

Flexibility is at the centre of implementing "different strokes for different folks." By exercising the option to change your style of supervising your crew based on their individual performance, you will create positive results with employee retention. Like communication, flexibility is easier said than done and here's where that bungee cord in your kitbag proves a valuable tool. Like all intrepid voyagers, the captain can weather any storm with the right people on board. Keeping the right people on board involves treating them with respect for their individual style and needs.

## Chapter Tools

# Bridging the Generation Gaps

## *Values, Motivation and Communication*

|  | **Veterans** | **Boomers** | **Gen X** | **Gen Y** |
|---|---|---|---|---|
| **Key Work Values** | Dedication & Loyalty<br><br>Respect hierarchy<br><br>Do whatever it takes | Live to work<br><br>Seek consensus<br><br>Seek personal gratification | Seek work/life balance<br><br>Entrepreneurial<br><br>Goal oriented | Work to live<br><br>Goal & team Oriented<br><br>Seek to work on their own terms |
|  |  |  |  |  |
| **More likely to be motivated when...** | Their experience is valued and respected | They feel valued and needed | They are valued and involved | They work with a supportive team |
|  |  |  |  |  |
| **Most likely to prefer to communicate...** | In person or formally in writing | Directly or in person<br><br>phone or voicemail | Directly or indirectly, immediately<br><br>Email, phone or text message, voicemail | Instantly<br><br>IM, text message, phone |

By: Dynamic HR Solutions Inc. Used with permission

References for this chart include:

Zemke, Ron; Raines, Claire; Filipczak, Bob. *Generations at Work: Managing the Clash of Veterans, Boomers, Xers, and Nexters in Your Workplace.* New York, N.Y.: American Management Association, 2000.

Sago, Brad. *Uncommon Threads: Mending the Generation Gap at Work, Executive Update,* July 2000

Hammill, Greg. *Mixing and Managing Four Generations of Employees,* Accessed 2007 (online publication), http://www.fdu.edu/newspubs/ magazine/05ws/generations.htm

# Human Resource Solutions Project
# Retain Productive People

## Support Cultural Harmony

Educate all staff about cultural sensitivity.
Provide orientation on Canadian work culture, while recognizing different cultural norms.
Introduce new workers personally to existing staff.
Offer some flexibility in working hours for the observance of cultural traditions.

## Facilitate Open Communication

Find common ground, but accommodate differences.
Invite and provide frequent feedback to and from employees.
Use plain language for communication, orientation as well as clarifying expectations.

## Provide a Supportive Environment

Create a buddy/mentor system for orientation and exchange of knowledge.
Carry out team-building activities that instill a sense of belonging for all employees.
Support professional development opportunities for newcomers' long-term integration and growth.

> *From: Victoria Immigrant and Refugee Centre Society*
> Used with permission
> (For more information about the Human Resource Solutions Project, please contact
> 250-361-9433 ext: 244 or 245)

# Chapter 6

## The 5 Things Your Crew Really Wants From You
### *Hint: It's not About the Gold*

*"…love the job I'm in. It fits my skills and values and I'm treated like gold which is actually more important to me than the gold…"*
- Anonymous survey respondent

You may think that the primary motivation for employees is the checks they take home bi-weekly and deposit into their accounts. But in fact, recent research and my own poll as well as my experience over years of working with clients in career transition show that there are several other factors-totally unrelated to money that are far more important in employees' minds. Five things employees want are:

- To know that their employer cares about them.

- To have the opportunity to grow and develop.

- To work within a culture that is respectful and supportive.

- To have balance between work and life.

- To work where relationships are positive.

In the following chapter we will take each of these topics in turn and discuss their importance, and ways you can implement them in your own business.

Once the data from our surveys in Canada were compiled we determined there was some overlap with the employee engagement research conducted by Towers Perrin, as well as with numerous other reports that circulate in the halls of human resources. The Towers-Perrin report: *Closing the Engagement Gap: A Road Map for Driving Superior Business Performance* provides readers with some hard truths about leadership and the workplace. The good news is that employee engagement-the level at which employees bring their discretionary effort to work can be developed. Towers-Perrin also provides us with data that indicates employees *want* to be engaged at work₁. This is powerful and compelling data, but I just had to have my own numbers, to see for myself what I had already learned over the years of running a business with 32 staff.

The survey I conducted, along with interviews with successful companies, corroborates (albeit on a smaller scale) the findings of many human resources research studies about what employees really want from their jobs, from their immediate supervisor and from the company. It surprises many people that money is *not* at the top of the list as a driver of employee retention. As employers, we keep throwing money at the problem of employee retention. Alternatively, we throw in more benefits, or up the number of what I call "silly perks" like pool tables and cappuccino machines. Pool tables and cappuccino machines have their place, but don't copy someone else's perks and try to make them fit for your culture. That's when they become silly.

Jennifer Hawes at ColdStar Freight Systems shares a funny story about her decision to share the air miles that the company had accumulated. "It seemed like such a good idea," she mused. "I thought it would be something employees would want. I tried to divide up the air miles between employees. After all, we had over a million air miles." Soon, chaos and dissension, even resignations resulted. "How on earth do you fairly distribute air miles?" Jennifer asked. It had seemed like a great idea for a perk, but was so poorly implemented that it was near impossible to distribute the booty fairly. On a tight ship, in a storm, the crew *has to* get along, and anything that causes unrest among crew can only cause unrest for the ship as a whole. I can only imagine this crew dueling it out with swords while Jennifer and husband, Kelly are at the helm and trying to change sails.

I shudder at the memory of one particularly disastrous perk that I tried early in my consulting practice. I implemented a contest to increase the number of referrals to job openings that would assist our clients. Employees would track and post potential job openings that were collected through their contacts. These job openings, often from what is referred to in employment circles as "the hidden job market" created increased opportunities for our clients. I had only a dozen or so staff at the time, and I had read a book about creating perks and opportunities for sales teams and others to perform. The carrot in this contest was a weekend trip away to a wonderful spa resort-a trip for two. What could have been a friendly contest turned into a human resources nightmare. Complaints erupting in the staff room, accusations of unfair practices and lots of "cold shoulder" communication became prevalent shortly after implementing this "perk." While the basic, positive premise of reward being tied to performance was in place, the whole "team" notion-of which we were most proud-almost disintegrated. Lesson learned: If you operate as a team, but reward individual performance, don't expect a high performing team. You'll read more about teams in chapter eight.

And what do employees want from their leader? They want the same things that their customers do! Employees join great companies and leave bad managers. This well-known cliché of business rings truer in challenging economic and labor markets. The *Number One reason* employees in my survey said they had left their jobs was because they were unhappy with their supervisors.

## The Number One thing employees want…

According to countless reputable surveys in our survey and in interviews, they said they want₂:

## ...To Know That Their Employer Cares About Them!

Granted this takes time and effort and planning. But most of all it takes genuine commitment on the part of supervisors-oh yes, and a desire and natural affinity to care about people. It takes time and practice, but it takes even more time to keep replacing staff and when that labor market pool runs dry there really won't be anyone to do the work that needs to be done. It is imperative that a supervisor shows concern for an employee. We are not talking here about hour-long pity sessions, but a simple, "How are you? How was your holiday? How did your son do with his little league tryouts?" This is so simple, but easy to forget when we get "Busy With The Important Stuff."

You already know that this caring works with customers. One caring inquiry, "Mrs. Smith, how did that paint color work for you in your living room?" goes a long way to establish customer loyalty. Have you gone into a paint store lately? Did you get that kind of caring inquiry? Maybe you are going to the wrong paint store! Supervisors, managers and CEOs need to connect, connect and connect. Employees may be starving for human connection. However, don't connect if you really don't care. Employees (and customers) can see right through the sham when the genuineness is missing. Learn to care. You can learn to get better at caring, and sometimes it takes understanding that the care you or your managers show to employees comes back to you in trust and in loyalty. The "My company is too big to check in on employees, it's not like they need babysitting," response doesn't cut it as an excuse to skip this important step in retaining good employees.

In an interview in her office, Jennifer Hawes at ColdStar Freight Systems described how she makes sure that her 105 employees have connected to at least one other staff member within their first few weeks at work. She uses this as a benchmark to ensure that no one is working in isolation. After each new employee's first few weeks on the job, Jennifer sits down in an informal meeting with the new employee to determine their connections in the company. How can employees not get the message that this employer cares as much about the person, as a person, as she does about their role as an employee? In a recent review of their benefits plan, the company reduced the number of hours that an employee has to work in order to qualify for the company benefits package. This was a costly item, but Jennifer said that it was important to staff and management felt that it was worth the extra cost in terms of employee satisfaction (and we know that satisfaction is synonymous with retention.)

A captain who provides opportunities for his crew to have some input into decisions that affect them is demonstrating care and concern for the work environment that employees operate within. Caring about employees doesn't have to cost money. Providing opportunities for input into the decision-making process is just another way to ensure that employees have a voice. From our survey, 43.4 percent of employees said that they were either somewhat dissatisfied or extremely dissatisfied with their ability to provide input into issues that affected their jobs.

The next step after asking for input *has* to be follow-up. Jennifer explained how twice a year they hold an all-company staff meeting. "This is not a meeting where we yak at them," she said; instead, these meetings provide a true opportunity for input on issues that the company is wrestling with. Jennifer suggests mixing up the groups so that feedback teams encompass all parts of the organization from secretarial support to drivers to mechanics. It was at one such meeting that all of the staff helped to come up with the previously mentioned slogan and byline: *ColdStar Freight Systems-A Respectful and Passionate Company.* Suggestions offered by employees are reported in the company newsletter, so that those who offer suggestions know exactly what has happened with their input. It is not about saying "yes" to all suggestions, that's obviously not possible, but employees know what happened with their suggestions and why or why not their idea was or could be implemented.

Compare Jennifer's effective methodology with the following example that was offered by one of the survey respondents. The survey allowed an opportunity for additional comments and some of them were very revealing!

**For example:**

"I was employed with a small Internet Service Provider. Management would frequently assign me to perform very menial tasks and work on projects unlikely to become a success, all without ever first consulting me. I was the only person in the company with the information to form a well-reasoned opinion on any of the projects."

"In my first few months, I enjoyed my job immensely. It was very clear exactly where they needed me, and I was able to perform my tasks with a level of proficiency and was able to complete job orders of magnitude beyond what they had seen in the past. I set up a web server, email server, file server, and streaming media server. I built numerous client websites including the company's own, using my own designs and integrating popular industry applications like message board systems and content management applications. Unfortunately, after a while it became clear to my boss, there was very little he couldn't use me for."

"Before long I found myself in charge of everything from removing viruses and adware from PCs around the office, to troubleshooting broken CD burners, to installing printers... right up to stuffing envelopes with invoices for our clients. Rarely did I get the chance to complete any of the larger tasks one would expect from a database administrator or network administrator, the roles I largely identified myself with, much less a web developer, the role I was officially titled under with the company."

"The fact that no one discussed the plan with me in advance, coupled with the realization that my boss and everyone else at the meeting felt completely comfortable with even small-scale projects taking months to complete, left me concluding that my dissatisfaction with my job was unlikely to change any time soon... After finally realizing that my concerns were unlikely to be addressed, I believe I did the company a favor in eventually stopping all efforts to complete the website, and instead moving to tie up some of the loose ends I had been left with over the course of the last few months, before I finally notified the company that I was quitting."

**And other respondent comments:**
"Regardless of the type of job, it is the manager/supervisor that really makes a difference. Having someone who is not supportive, who belittles you and does not give proper training or assistance really makes a difference in your experience. The atmosphere and fellow employees can be your ideal working conditions but without an appropriate manager, it doesn't matter. Even though my job was really demanding

it was also enjoyable because of my relationships with who I worked with."

"I have recently started a new job, and it is outstanding. The environment is very supportive, and I am working in a field that gives me a great deal of personal satisfaction."

"My main area of concern is the change of management and of what I perceive as a lack of competence in the managers I deal with, even though it is not a major part of my contract. It does have an effect… I am actually quite happy with the job itself. And part of me will be upset to leave the position as I have really made it my own."

The best news about increasing employee input is that the type of input and increased communication between management and employees is relatively simple to implement. When asked to suggest one piece of advice for the small and medium size employer who is struggling with employee retention issues, Jennifer didn't hesitate to offer:

*"Canvass your key people. Find out about the issues that are affecting them, and what can be done to improve performance."*

After the air miles mess, Jennifer said that she now brings new ideas to a small group of managers to test it out. Then if it flies she brings it to a larger group of key employees for testing and input. She adds, "Not only do staff have input on these ideas that will impact their work lives, but I also avoid the type of experience like the air miles gift that became a nightmare."

## Employees Want the Opportunity to Grow and Develop

In our survey, nearly half of the respondents were either somewhat dissatisfied or extremely dissatisfied with their access to training programs. The opportunity for training is a direct reflection both of the employer caring for the employee and in managing performance. Well-planned and well-executed training is a win-win situation for even the smallest employer. With technology growing and changing rapidly, the shelf life of most careers is surprisingly short, and without training, employees are falling behind. According to the December 2008 Times Colonist newspaper article, by Eric Beachesne, Canadian employers fall short in comparison with twelve other countries in their spending on training. Quoting from a Proudfoot Consulting report, Beachesne noted that:

*"…while Canadian companies identify a skills shortage as the number one roadblock to efficiency improvements, at the same time they provide one of the lowest levels of training."*

If Canadian companies are among the least likely to offer training to employees, it should not be a surprise that GDP is adversely affected, and on a micro scale, small business is lagging in efficiency. But in hard times, it is often the training budget that small businesses hack at to control expenses. A double-edged sword such as minimal training and reduced productivity can be a powder keg on board a ship.

"Recruitment, retention and morale are closely linked to effective training and internal communications," says Jon Wylie, Proudfoot's managing director in Canada. In difficult economic climates, when the temptation is there to throw training overboard, a wise captain instead investigates and assesses crew training needs. And a good assessment means far more than asking, "What training would crew like?" It means being strategic and finding gaps in competency. Such training may be formal or informal and may come in the form of mentoring or coaching programs, or possibly involve job rotation (also a flexibility tool) or sharing industry best practices.

Do your employees know about advancement opportunities? Are they aware of a career track within your company? Developing employees is a fine example of a double win – it's good for employees, and it's particularly good for business.

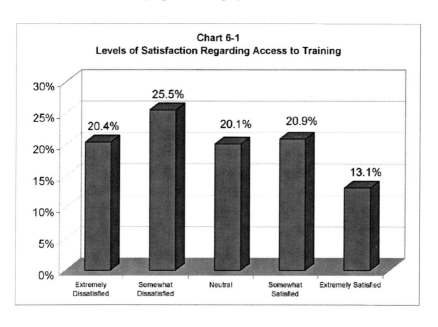

# Employees Want a Respectful and Supportive Workplace Culture

Respect is what we are all seeking at some level or another. The opposite, a lack of respect, undermines nearly everything to which we may aspire.

So... no interrupting, belittling, degrading-all indicators of showing disrespect-seems so reasonable. And the good news from our survey: employees expressed satisfaction with employers' respecting differences as 25 percent reported they were satisfied and 33 percent were extremely satisfied with workplace cultures that were free of harassment and bullying.

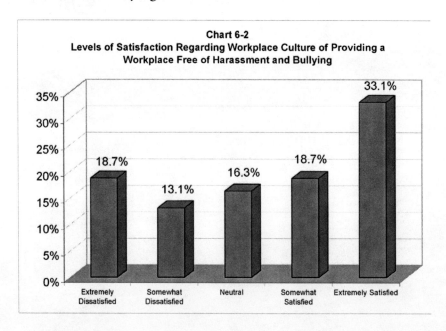

Chart 6-2
Levels of Satisfaction Regarding Workplace Culture of Providing a
Workplace Free of Harassment and Bullying

Once you've mastered respecting differences and supporting a culture that is free of harassment and bullying there is still work to be done. Respondents to our survey indicated much dissatisfaction with supporting staff that failed to encourage employees to develop and reach their potential. In fact, nearly half of the respondents were either dissatisfied or extremely dissatisfied in this area of workplace culture.

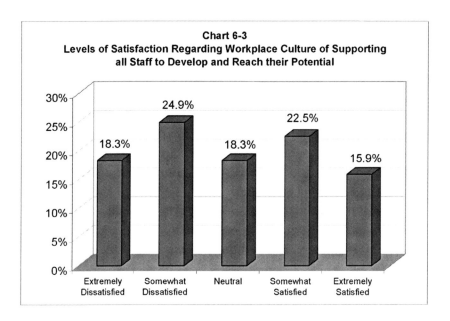

**Chart 6-3**
**Levels of Satisfaction Regarding Workplace Culture of Supporting all Staff to Develop and Reach their Potential**

A captain would do well to create a work environment that allowed all crew to reach their full potential. How else can a ship perform in day to day operations, let alone survive in a storm? Developing and reaching potential goes beyond the training mentioned earlier. It goes beyond the values alignment and centers on creating opportunities for challenge and advancement. It's about filling the gap between where a crew member is currently operating and where they could be. And it takes a tremendous amount of attention to where the crew member is now and where they aspire to be.

We all have self-actualization goals, what Abraham Maslow indicates is the human desire at the top of the human needs pyramid. Maslow's hierarchy indicates reaching this potential as a motivating force for most of your crew[3]. For crew to reach their potential, it is the captain's duty to clear the decks of obstacles that stop or hinder individual (and organizational) progress. Here's where you need to unpack those sensible deck shoes from your kit bag, get out to where the action is, and pay close attention. Look around your ship. How many levels of approval are required for any one crew member to take action on any one decision? How many rules are in place? What messages do these rules send to your employees about your trust in them? What level of decision making does any one crew member hold?

Kouzes and Posner's book, *The Leadership Challenge* (now in its fourth edition) outlines five fundamental practices of leadership. Their work is based on what may well be the most extensive research ever conducted on the topic of effective leadership practices. One of the practices they highlight is entitled: "Enable Others to Act." This is the heart of developing crew to reach their potential. Kouzes and Posner outline the values of creating collaborative partnerships with all constituents, including employees.

*" Leaders strengthen others when they give their power away, when they make it possible for constituents to exercise choice and discretion, when they develop competence to excel, when they assign critical tasks, and when they offer visible support.[4] "*

A captain has to have his sensible deck shoes on to create this type of environment. He has to be at the mast along with his crew to know the development needs of the crew and to begin to implement ways to enhance them. Captains often jump in too frequently, doing everything themselves rather than effectively delegating (and thereby empowering) their employees. As Captain Greg Sager says "The captain gets into his role too much on most ships. They're orchestrating every aspect of the jobs. A captain has to stand back and watch them (employees) operate the business. A captain has to relax- ultimately you need someone to steer the ship, but the more the captain is involved in always steering the ship, the harder it is for crew when they're needed to take on that job."

## Employees Want Work and Family Balance

This is especially true of our "Generation Y" employees, for whom work comes second to life. The kit bag's bungee cord comes into play here, and is a key tool to be able to exercise the necessary flexibility. It is not an easy road to continuously offer flexibility, but in the long run, the employees are happier and their levels of engagement are enhanced. In sailing terms, an upwind and a downwind of give and take is the key to flexibility. Give and take is *not* about counting how many IOUs are in the bank of flexible work terms, but in the day-to-day creative problem solving when work and life, or work and family collide.

I remember one young mom who was working for me. She was a single parent with three children in elementary school. The week before school started she was reviewing her schedule with me, outlining specific tasks she was working on and deadlines that were approaching. When I asked her, "What are you doing coming in on the first day of school?" her surprised expression turned to a smile.

"Can I take the morning off?"

"Well, with three children to get to their new classes, you'd better not be here on the first day of school," I replied. This was no saintly act on my part, nor was it entirely altruistic. I knew that this person was a star player on my team, a talented and conscientious member of my crew. I am also a mother, and I know the enormous challenges of that first day of school, and how important it is for most moms to participate in first day events.

To allow the time off, but more importantly, to initiate the conversation, provided evidence that I cared about this staff and her family and about the balance of work and life. This staff member had on many, many occasions provided me with evidence that she was fully engaged and committed to her job. I had been on the receiving end of this employee's commitment and flexibility as she worked through a number of deadline projects. It's an upwind and a downwind journey-sometimes you're working with elements that help you to be more productive, and sometimes, it's the employee who benefits from the flexibility. Take any opportunity that you may have to demonstrate flexibility as it is so important to all of your crew.

Most successful technology companies, whose employee base typically is made up to Generation 'X' and Generation 'Y' workers-are exercising some type of work flexibility. And in our survey, 30 percent of respondents indicated they were extremely satisfied with the flexible work arrangements at their workplace. Flexible work environments are becoming more of the norm, and according to Human Resources experts at World at Work more than twenty-nine million Americans work remotely from their offices and an estimated one hundred million will do so in the next 3 years[5].

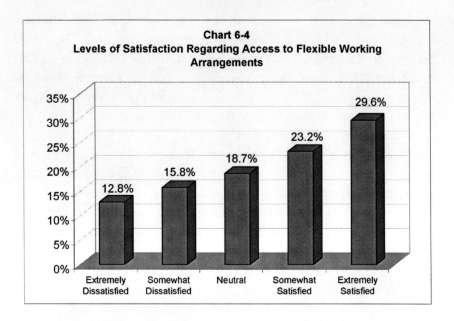

**Chart 6-4**
**Levels of Satisfaction Regarding Access to Flexible Working Arrangements**

Some of our respondents' comments about flexibility:

…"worked fulltime for over 17 yrs, asked to work part time and they flatly refused…don't like part time employees."

…"Main reason for leaving was medical; was not able to 'physically' return to work after major operation, i.e., needed longer recovery time, and employer could not grant it."

At least a couple of times, I have also been on the receiving end of flexibility afforded me when I most needed it. In both instances, it made the difference between staying and leaving. ( And in both instances it was all about sailing !) In the first example, I was in my twenties and working for an employment agency. My husband and I had spent two years building our 39-foot sailboat and as launch day approached, it was clear that my workload would not allow for a much-needed holiday. However, my manager recognized the intense effort that had gone into building this boat (my husband and I each averaged 30 hours per week on top of full time work over the two-year period) and she afforded me one whole day off to celebrate the launch. The wonderful surprise was that the entire office closed for the lunch hour, and a sign was posted on the door: "Out to Launch." This enabled all of the staff to celebrate with me.

In the second example, I had been contracting with Women's Enterprise Centre for several years, and had recently come aboard as an employee. Our sailboat had sold, and we had accepted a trade. The only catch was that we had a 1600 km journey to sail the new boat home, and time was of the essence. It was October, and the weather window to get that boat (and us) home safely was closing in. I didn't have any holidays accumulated with my new employer but was afforded the flexibility of time off without pay in order to complete this important journey.

Life does get in the way of business, and leaders are challenged with balancing the task at hand with the long-term employee relationships. In my experience, the more flexibility a captain can manage, the greater the level of loyalty. It's an upwind and a downwind journey!

## Employees want to work where relationships are positive

There's a highly entertaining IKEA television advertisement that portrays a middle-aged man coming home from work screaming, "I hate my job! I hate my boss!" The man's ire is silenced by the experience of entering the threshold of a beautiful IKEA kitchen (Well, at least his wife is soothed watching him in the beautiful kitchen.) But it's really disconcerting to think that such rage is more common that it needs to be.

> In fact, statistics tell us that the highest percentage of heart attacks occur on Mondays[6.] Going to work can be very stressful and in workplaces where the relationship tensions are high, often the turnover rate is also high.

Once again, there are encouraging results in our survey. Over 28 percent of respondents were extremely satisfied with their current relationships with immediate supervisors, and a further 23 percent were somewhat satisfied with those relationships. We know good people join good companies and leave bad supervisors. This well-known observation shows up in nearly every discussion on the topic of employee retention. Our survey did not depart from this common knowledge; in fact, 27 percent of those who had quit jobs within the past 5 years said their primary reason for quitting was that they were unhappy with their supervisors. While it could be argued that "unhappy with supervisor" is a somewhat ambiguous term, it clearly indicates the importance of good relationships with direct supervisors. After more than 25 years in the human resources field, I am convinced that most people do not quit their jobs without due consideration. The stress of being unhappy with one's immediate supervisor takes a serious toll and often forces such a decision.

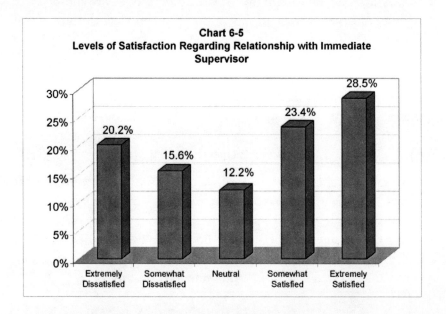

As a business owner, you may sometimes celebrate when an employee makes the move to quit. There are times, when the match or fit between job and employee is off, and everyone benefits when the employee leaves. It's also important to reflect on *who* is leaving the company. In order to get a solid handle on understanding employee retention issues the question has to be asked, "Why did any particular staff member leave?" This information is typically obtained via exit interviews. Remember that exit interviews require a level of courage and listening. Over half of our survey respondents were aged 40 to 59 and most described themselves as skilled and experienced. They quit jobs in a huge cross-section of industries and over 22 percent of those who quit had been with the company over 5 years when they left. That translates into a lot of talent jumping ship! (See Appendix 1 for survey respondent data)

If relationship issues are a primary cause, the root must be explored more carefully. In our next chapter we will look at asking questions to get more facts, not only about what is not working, but what *is* working. Armed with this information, a captain can concentrate on why crew stay- and that's a positive lens from which to review employee retention.

## But What About the *Gold*?

Isn't paying a higher wage a way to keep employees on board? What we know about pay scales is that the higher wages are a factor for attracting crew to your ship but not necessarily for keeping them there! In fact, only 16 percent of our respondents quit their job due to unsatisfactory pay level. And less than 1 percent quit because of an unsatisfactory benefits schedule. However, all things considered, we cannot leave the gold equation out of consideration in employee retention. Zach North, our coffee wizard at Bean Around the World, stated:

*"I love that we're not paid minimum wage. Minimum wage says to me-if you could pay any less you would."*

When I hit the 5-year milestone in my business, I initiated a 22 percent pay increase for staff. I had conducted some industry analysis and wanted my staff to be at the highest possible end of the scale. That same year at our annual retreat, we were reviewing the year. Our facilitator for the day encouraged us to review the highs and lows, the accomplishments, the most salient events from an organizational and personal perspective. To my surprise, not one person noted the pay increase! Not that the pay increase wasn't needed or appreciated, or necessary. It just wasn't on anyone's radar as a highlight. What was highlighted at that retreat included the professional accomplishments, the pride in exceeding our targets on every contract, the personal satisfaction of work done well and the amount of fun we had had doing it all. Our annual retreat was a celebration of individual and group pride - it was more than gold.

So, in this chapter we have looked at some of the main factors in employee satisfaction in the workplace. These are the things that make people stay! And according to my survey, my years in the human resources field and from other industry research, the five main points are:

- Demonstrating care for employees.

- Offering a workplace that is respectful and supportive.

- Providing training and development opportunities for staff.

- Ensuring a workplace that promotes and demonstrates positive working relationships.

- Providing flexibility for work and life balance.

These are things that you may be able to implement in varying degrees and over time in your business. They may provide a foundation for future change. Some of the factors that you will want to consider in implementing changes may be reviewed in the "A VICTORY acronym that is outlined in Chapter Tools. If these are the things that are important to your employees, taking action will produce positive results. After all, a happy crew makes for a happy voyage, and most importantly contributes to overall employee retention.

# Chapter Tools

Some examples of workplace flexibility:

- Part-time

- Flex-time

- Unpaid leave of absence

- Employee chooses preferred hours

- Family leave days

- Tele-commuting

- Part-time tele-commuting

- Job sharing

- Compressed work week

- Job rotation

- Paid time off for volunteer work

- Job shadowing opportunities

A captain can effectively apply any of the above solutions, based on employee need and organizational goals. Not all employees are suited to flexible work solutions, and not all organizations are designed to incorporate many of these options, but the act of reviewing and analyzing options demonstrates that the flexibility factor is alive and well on your ship.

Questions to review before implementing a flexible work option:

- Can the employee work without supervision?

- What type of environment works best for this employee?

- How will the flexible work arrangement affect the work of others?

- Have I drafted a memorandum of understanding that outlines both parties' expectations?

- Does this arrangement meet my province or state labor laws?

- Operationally, how will the work be delivered and scheduled?

- Can the employee complete the same amount of work (i.e. in a compressed work week?)

- How will customers be affected?

- What would be a reasonable pilot period to test out any option?

- How will I evaluate the results of a pilot period?

- What would be the anticipated results of a failed pilot?

Here is Vincent Barabba and Gerald Zaltman's A VICTORY$_7$ acronym. Taking into consideration, all of these factors will help a manager, a supervisor, a leader to consider changes based on a holistic view of the organization and its readiness for change.

A=Ability

What resources does your organization have to manage change? What about you? What tools from your kit bag will help? Plan ahead for what you may need in assessing ability and include it in your action plan in chapter 10.

V=Values

Is there compatibility between management's attitudes and behaviors and practices with the values, cultural norms and attitudes of the change? A perfect match would be implementing flex time on a ship that values work-life balance.

I=Idea/Information

Complex information about the change should be provided as simply as possible. The reason for the change must be understood by all, at all levels of the organization. Map it out and include everyone by encouraging questions, ideas and ensuring clarity at all levels.

C=Circumstances

What factors in the organization affect the acceptance and implementation of the change? Has your ship just recruited all new officers? Are there other special circumstances to consider with regards to implementing this change?

T=Timing

How ready is the organization to implement the proposed change? Are current weather conditions to your advantage? What's brewing up ahead? Have you just traveled through a storm?

O=Obligation

Do relevant decision makers and champions perceive the need for change? Are they ready and committed? How much of the change is "should" and how much is "want to"?

R=Resistance

What is the level of resistance to change-generally and with regards to this one? What tools do you have in place to overcome or manage this resistance? Openness and honesty are key considerations here. Manage the resistance from a place of understanding, then being understood.

Y=Yield

What are the benefits of the change for those who are asked to approve or implement it? Can you answer the question from many perspectives "What's in it for me?"

# Chapter 7

## The Courage to Ask the Questions
## and Hear the Answers

*"Men go abroad to wonder the heights of mountains, at the huge waves of the sea, at the long courses of the rivers, at the vast compass of the ocean, at the circular motions of the stars; and they pass by themselves without wondering."* - St. Augustine

Perhaps we "pass by" ourselves without wondering because it is actually easier to ask questions about the incomprehensible infinity of space than it is to ask deep questions of ourselves. These are the hard questions, and the ones from which we have the most to learn. Questions are how we learn. Ask a question, get an answer; and grow in your knowledge. This is true in all learning arenas and is no different when running your business.

Dr. Leo Buscaglia, educator and author, addressed a group of educators in Victoria, BC in 1977. I still remember much of what this amazing educator had to say. He told us that children in grade 1 ask questions 10 times more often than children in grade 3. Somewhere along the line of learning we stop asking questions. Our sense of curiosity is still there but we grow into adults and into leaders and we ask fewer questions₁.

Why does this happen? Part of it is certainly a natural fear of the response we might receive. You know the routine: someone says, "Tell me what you think, how am I doing? Is there anything I could do better? Don't be afraid to tell me straight-my friends do and I can take it." Then you proceed with some insights or observations or suggestions for improvement, and the employee or friend or colleague gives you the "how-dare–you" stare and then severs communication with you entirely. Who hasn't experienced such a dysfunctional conversation? On the opposite end is the employer who asks, "How am I doing?" but who has little regard for the answer and writes it off to "that employee is just dissatisfied no matter what." In this chapter we'll delve into some of the questions and practices that can help you to learn and to create more awareness about what works best for you and for your crew.

I'll start with a question:

Still got that mirror in your kit bag? Here is another place that you really need it. Courage plays an enormous role in asking the questions that will shine the spotlight on potential problems. Remember Jennifer's number one suggestion to employers who are wrestling with employee retention issues? "Canvass your key people." I particularly liked her choice of words, considering the role of canvas on a sailing ship!

There are countless ways to take the temperature on board a ship. The engine room has gauges for everything from oil pressure to engine temperature to battery-charging capacity. The efficiency of the sails can be measured in speed, and the overall performance on an offshore passage can be measured in nautical miles per day. But what about the crew? How do we take *their* temperature? In a small or medium-sized company, employee turnover rates are one telltale sign. Keep in mind that the number 1 reason that employees in our survey quit was that they were not happy with their supervisor. That's a hard truth for most leaders to swallow. It's easy to dismiss it by generalizing that "They're probably unhappy with *all* supervisors." A wise captain will look more carefully at the reasons, and compare them with overall retention rates. If you're going through crew like you're going through the ship's stash of sea biscuits, all signs point to a change in direction.

Start your journey with a desire to gain clarity about how you're doing as a manager. This part of the voyage is not always easy, but it's always intensely rewarding.

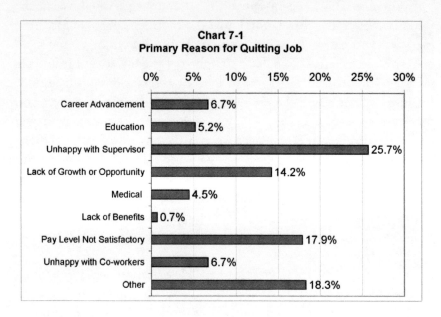

The highest percentage of respondents in our survey indicated that "unhappy with supervisor" was the primary reason for quitting their job. The extensive Towers-Perrin research discovered some similar findings in the vein of retention issues. They reported the overall number 1 retention driver as the organization's reputation as a great place to work and close behind, at number 3, a "good relationship with supervisor[2]." How do you know what is happening in your organization? How do you know if your employees see this as a good place to work or whether or not they have good relationships with their supervisors? In other words, how do you begin to take the temperature? The first step is to consider *what* you want to know, and how you will go about collecting the information. Depending on your time and financial resources, and any specific query you may have you might consider:

- For a general temperature or climate assessment: an employee satisfaction survey.

- For increased understanding of all supervisors' effectiveness (including your own) as leaders: a comprehensive 360-degree leadership evaluation.

- For feedback on new policy implementation or planning or a new project proposal, or changes to existing procedures: an informal poll of key stakeholders or key employees.

- For determining gaps in knowledge, talent or skill needed for business improvement or growth: a training needs analysis.

- For determining employee-ready access to assistance and support: A questionnaire that indicates employee knowledge of where to get assistance for specific concerns or questions.

Whichever tool you decide on (some samples and recommended reading are included in chapter tools) it is worth noting that some surveys can go sideways and do more harm than good if not handled with respect and honesty. I had to sail backwards after a disastrous survey that I used with staff some years ago. We were launching a new project and I asked staff to complete a survey on their perceived needs for equipment, materials, new computers and other capital cost items. Staff completed the survey and shortly afterwards, we cancelled the project due to unforeseen circumstances. While the survey had been launched with honesty and truth, it had also created expectations that were unrealistic. I had not submitted any parameters or contingency explanations in the survey, and rightly so, staff assumed that they were all getting whatever they listed as new and needed equipment and materials. The sailing backward would not have been necessary had I included a more comprehensive explanation upfront. As in the example in a previous chapter about the dysfunctional communication that can occur *after* asking the questions, it is imperative that a company seek the information only if they are sincerely interested in hearing the answers. This can be a painful but equally effective growth opportunity.

Additionally, the surveys, interviews, and polls are meaningless unless there is real intent to follow up on them. No employee wants to be surveyed, only to wonder evermore what the results were--or worse yet, wonder what management is intending to do with the results. This is particularly important when asking for feedback and surveys related to performance issues. A manager or supervisor must then concentrate on the core characteristic of honesty in order to meet the crucial need to develop and maintain trust.

If you are willing and courageous enough to look in the mirror after the results of the survey and take steps to improve your own management or supervisory style, you will see results that will align with your business goals. You can only ever change yourself. And it's true. People around you will change when you do, but you can only change yourself.

A project prior to the 2nd year residency period for my master's degree required a 360-degree poll of my leadership style with 10 staff. I purposefully (and may I say bravely?) polled both those whose respect I knew I had, and those with whom I was struggling in our work relationship. The project helped me to realize that my level of competitiveness was seen as very high. It gave me cause for reflection. Why would others see me as highly competitive? I learned that my need to be "best" was overriding my efforts to learn more and my fear of failure was projected in a highly competitive "contest to be won" view of work. This increased knowledge helped me to take steps to become a more effective leader.

Improving performance didn't come easily and I asked others to help me in overcoming my need to be competitive at every opportunity. It was helpful and encouraging that staff consistently rated me as being able to inspire and motivate others and as having well-developed interpersonal skills, so I had these strengths to work with in developing my weaknesses. That's the beauty of good feedback, you have the opportunity to learn about both strengths and weaknesses and the two can work together in a concerted and conscious effort to be more effective. The gain was certainly worth the pain.

A more collaborative approach became the norm, even with former "competitors." I was invited to Toronto, Canada later that year to address a group of 550 Human Resources Development Canada managers to describe the implementation of a uniquely collaborative Community Services model which we had instigated and implemented through the support of a visionary and effective local HRDC manager.

The following proverb tells the tale of how things cannot change if we do not.

## A Proverb

A man, with his backpack on his back, was moving from one village to another. Along his journey he met a wise woman (Don't ask me how he knew she was a wise woman–maybe there was a signpost : wise woman ahead) but he did stop and he asked her, "What are the people like in the next town?"

"What were they like in the village you've just moved from?"she asked in response.

"Well, they were *not* very friendly, and there was no work. No one would give me work, and the neighbors were stingy and rude," the traveler said.

"I'm sorry to say that you'll find the exact same type of people in the new village." she offered.

The man carried on his way, disgruntled and weary.

Another man came upon this same woman in his journey from one village to the next. He asked her the same question, "What are the people like in the village ahead?" and the wise woman asked the identical question of this man, about the nature of the people in the previous village.

"Oh, the folks in my village were kind and helpful. They had no more work but have helped me to move ahead and suggested that there may be work in this next village. I hope that the people in this new village are as kind and thoughtful as in my last home."

The wise woman responded "I think you will find the exact same type of people in the new village."

The man carried on his way, hopeful and optimistic.

(Original source of this proverb unknown)

What we can learn from this proverb is the value of taking a good look at our own reflection and how we are perceived by employees. You can only change yourself, not others. Start with understanding how others see their jobs, your own performance and roads to improvement. If you use a survey, do the right things with your survey results. Communicate your intentions to staff and don't make promises that either you cannot keep, or that you have no intention of keeping. As Jennifer at ColdStar explained, "What is most unique about our company is that we seek employees' input and ask their opinion on things we're struggling with. How are we doing in these areas? What could we do better? Then we *act* on the suggestions and report back to employees with intentions and results." It's a doable formula for any sized company, and it pays off in maintaining employees in the trucking industry, an industry that historically has extremely high turnover.

Once you've communicated results and intentions, it's time to go back to that mirror. I came across this poem by Dale Wimbrow in the late seventies when I was teaching a Lifeskills course. It is as relevant to business as it is on a personal note, twenty five years later.

> "The Guy in the Glass"
> When you get what you want in your struggle for pelf*,
> And the world makes you King for a day,
> Then go to the mirror and look at yourself,
> And see what that guy has to say.
> For it isn't your Father, or Mother, or Wife,
> Whose judgment upon you must pass.
> The feller whose verdict counts most in your life
> Is the guy staring back from the glass.
> He's the feller to please, never mind all the rest,
> For he's with you clear up to the end,
> And you've passed your most dangerous, difficult test
> If the guy in the glass is your friend.
> You may be like Jack Horner and "chisel" a plum,
> And think you're a wonderful guy,
> But the man in the glass says you're only a bum
> If you can't look him straight in the eye.
> You can fool the whole world down the pathway of years,

And get pats on the back as you pass,
But your final reward will be heartaches and tears
If you've cheated the guy in the glass[3].

How you see yourself and the level of care and respect that you have for yourself is often reflected in those with whom you work most closely. This is the Kouzes and Posner practice referred to as "modeling the way." Managers who have healthy levels of positive self-regard may see this reflected in high levels of staff retention. Steven J. Stein in his book, *Make Your Workplace Great* says:

> *"High self-regard leaders (who know their strengths and weaknesses) project the kind of confidence (and humility) that is more likely to make people want to stay with the organization[4]."*

But what if you're not there yet? What does a captain do to learn these things? Firstly, the best news is that high self-regard and self-awareness are learnable. Just as you may offer coaching services to your employees for their self-development, so too can a captain develop these attributes through management coaching. Management coaching may be provided on-site, or off-site, via telephone, or in-person. Coaching in the corporate world and in the small business world is available through certified coaching consultants and consulting companies. Right Management and Towers-Perrin are just two examples of leading companies providing coaching services designed to enhance organizational performance. Before embarking on a coaching program be sure to take the time to identify what you are hoping to achieve. What tangible results are you seeking? The more specific your goals for coaching, the easier it will be to help you to decide on an appropriate match. Not surprising, professional coaching companies can help you to quickly realize your return on investment. Coaching improves your performance; it will also improve your bottom line. Some resources for coaching are included in Chapter Tools.

Monty Ravlich, President of Sanjel Corporation describes in his CBC radio interview the process of management coaching as being "a bit like psychoanalysis." For years, as a young and successful president of a growing company, he said that he often misinterpreted his own behavior, that he made decisions based on his reality. One example Ravlich related was when he offered employees a weekend away for a staff retreat. When staff did not respond with delight and appreciation he was confused, until he realized that he saw this benefit from his own perspective, which included, at the time, having no children. Staff had had to make extensive plans and preparations to spend a weekend away from their families. Ravlich dove into management coaching and attributes it as one of the success factors in growing his company from a two-truck operation to a 1,000-employee international company. "A rewarding and humbling experience" he says[5].

Management coaching may be an effective and even life-changing tool if the coaching match is suitable for your personal style and development needs. In her book *Coaching Corporate MVPs*, Margaret Butteriss interviewed over 20 corporations regarding coaching practices and a variety of views on the matching process were presented. Everything from the "chemistry" in the match, to the levels of trust, respect and style are offered as signposts for making an effective coaching match[6]. In our changing world of work, some of the styles we may have used in the past are less effective carrying us into the future. A sample of style choices is included in chapter tools and provides an excellent comparison of possibly outdated styles with more effective choices.

Mentoring is another way to develop skills needed to lead others effectively. A mentor match can involve both a formal and informal relationship. It is important to note that mentoring is different than coaching and may be implemented in a variety of ways. Formalized business mentoring programs are available in most urban centers, through business and industry associations, human resources associations or business networking groups. Did you know that you can choose anyone in the world to be your mentor? Now, they may not know that they are your mentor. A mentor is someone you admire, and you can learn from that mentor just by studying them, examining what and how they do things, and to use this admired person as a role-model. This type of informal or "ghost" mentoring is a common practice. You may have even practiced "ghost" mentoring without realizing that's where you learned certain business practices. Or, you may be a mentor to many people that you don't even know-others who are looking up to you for ways to approach problems or to communicate with others or to have fun at work, or for any number of the amazing characteristics that make up your reputation in business.

Regardless of what tools or strategies you implement to develop your skills, the act of involving employees is crucial for building skills and building trust. Openness and honesty are the ingredients of developing trust. Begin by asking some of these most courageous questions.

*How are things going for you in your job?*

This is a general, open-ended question that indicates to your employee that you are interested in their perspective on things, and invites feedback.

*What is one thing you'd like to change around here?*

This question provides a hint of what's not working, while allowing the employee to present some ideas without feeling like they are complaining.

*What is rewarded in this company?*

The answers to this question may surprise you. Remember it's not what you say; it's what others *see* being done. This is a reminder that you will always get more of what is rewarded, so this is an important question to point you to behaviors or actions that are in play.

*Where is there disagreement between you and others, or with me?*

O.K. the questions are getting tougher. Be patient. Listen carefully. Ask for clarification if needed. Don't jump to conclusions or prepare your response. No excuses or self-justification.

*How am I doing as your manager?*

Did we just cross the equator? Heat is turned up with this one and the same listening skills and patience are needed to hear an employee out. Remember that it is equally courageous of the employee to provide an answer to this question, as it is courageous for you to ask it- regardless if the feedback is negative or positive.

*When do you feel most fulfilled at work?*

The answer to this question will provide you with lots of information about employee values, desires and levels of satisfaction with the amount (or lack) of challenge.

*What one thing would make your job more rewarding?*

Sometimes a simple and inexpensive change can make all the

difference to an employee. Some of the most effective managers get in there and do the work of an employee for an hour, only to discover that a tool is missing or not working-but without either the communication strategy in place to discover it, or the opportunity to view the problem, it continues on as a festering problem.

*What are the factors that have made you stay in this job?*

Equally important as conducting exit interviews and determining why people leave their jobs, is finding out why they stay. This will give you information to continue some particular practices, or it may highlight some things you may have dismissed as "unimportant" that employees view as very important.

*Are you getting the degree of challenge that you need in your job?*

Never assume what level of challenge is comfortable for an individual employee. Some work best with routine and predictable work environments. Others require high levels of challenge, variety and new opportunities. Find out where employees fit and what it is that you can do to promote challenging opportunities where they are needed.

*What information and tools do you need to do your job?*

If your crew doesn't know where they're going, why they need to get there, and what expectations you have of them, and their tools are rusty and ineffective, how can they do their job? By asking this question, you'll be better able to implement strategies to enable crew to provide peak performance.

These are just a few of the questions that will help you to navigate through employee satisfaction issues. Through the use of feedback tools and the regular use of a mirror, you and your managers and supervisors will develop a healthy level of self awareness that fuels employee satisfaction and retention.

We've acknowledged that it's highly courageous to ask questions of your crew and it's highly courageous of your crew to provide feedback. Take steps, one at a time, to review and implement changes that will benefit employees, your company and you. The reward is in the results but the challenge is in the process. You and your crew can make course corrections along your journey and the positive, measurable results show up on your bottom line when you keep talent and experience on board. The winds of change are blowing your way and your ship is ready to take advantage of them. Time to take action, captain!

# Chapter Tools

Recommended Reading:

*The Leadership Challenge*: by Jim Kouzes and Barry Posner, Jossey-Bass Publishers, San Francisco , CA, Fourth Edition 2008

*The New Art of Managing People:* by Phil Hunsaker and Tony Alessandra, Free Press Publishers, a Division of Simon and Schuster, New York, NY 2008

*Good to Great:* by: Jim Collins, Random House Business, 2001

*Coaching Corporate MVPs* by: Margaret Butteriss, Right Management, Jossey-Bass Publishers, 2008

Feedback and Assessment Tools:

The Leadership Practices 360 Degree Feedback Tool is a well known and highly respected instrument that managers, supervisors and leaders from all walks of industry can utilize. To order or request information on The Leadership Practices Inventory, contact Pfeiffer (an imprint of Jossey-Bass) telephone at (800) 274-4434 or by fax at (800) 569-0443.

DISC: (Dominance; Influence; Steady; Compliance). This popular tool is a behaviorally-based assessment model, sometimes used as a communication tool. It measures your style and your "work adapted "style. For more information on DISC, contact Target Training International, telephone (800) 869-6908

Myers-Briggs Type Inventory is another well-known and respected instrument, used to help understand differences in the ways that people communicate, think and act. To order or request information contact: CPP Inc. and Davies-Black CA, (800) 624-1765 or email custserv@cpp.com

Coaching and Mentoring Resources
Right Management   http://www.right.com" www.right.com
Towers-Perrin   http://www.towersperrin.com" www.towersperrin.com
Coaches Canada   www.coaches Canada.com
International Coach Federation   http://www.coachfederation.org"
www.coachfederation.org
International Association of Coaching   www.certifiedcoach.org

Style Choices (with permission from: Being First Inc. www.beingfirst.com ) Use this chart to review a variety of styles and style alternatives. This chart offers a quick check on some of the ways that you may currently approach problems or situations, and some alternate, potentially more effective styles to consider. This may be a helpful chart in determining your style for matching with a mentor or coach to develop the most effective factors or characteristics as they relate to your business.

# Style Choices

| Style Choices | Factors | |
|---|---|---|
| **Being Proactive**<br>**vs**<br>**Being Reactive** | **Proactive:**<br>• Action-oriented<br>• Responsive to needs<br>• One step ahead<br>• Strategic | **Reactive:**<br>· Overwhelmed<br>· Crisis-oriented<br>· Passive |
| **Acting**<br>**Consciously**<br>**vs**<br>**Acting Out of**<br>**Habit** | **Consciousness:**<br>· Aware<br>· Scanning the situation<br>· Big picture focus<br>· Taking time to reflect | **Habit:**<br>· Denying what is<br>  happening<br>· Blind-sided<br>· Automatic pilot |
| **Taking**<br>**Responsibility**<br>**vs**<br>**Being Victimized** | **Responsibility:**<br>· Taking initiative to<br>  influence<br>· Creating better<br>· Circumstances<br>· Creating conditions for<br>  success | **Victimized:**<br>· Complaining, "If only…"<br>· Angry<br>· Unempowered to act<br>· Blaming |
| **Being Creative,**<br>**Taking Risks**<br>**vs**<br>**Using Routine** | **Creative, Risk-Taking:**<br>· Using innovation methods<br>· Freedom to explore<br>· Encouraging discovery<br>· Being adventurous<br>· Acting courageously | **Routinized:**<br>· Tradition-bound<br>· Bureaucratic procedures<br>· Doing what is expedient<br>  and familiar |
| **Being**<br>**Opportunity-**<br>**Focused**<br>**vs**<br>**Being Problem-**<br>**Focused** | **Opportunity Focused:**<br>· Pursuing value<br>· Freedom to learn<br>· Knowing the benefits<br>· Entrepreneurial | **Problem-Focused:**<br>· Burdened by concerns<br>· Status-quo oriented<br>· Pain-oriented |

| | | |
|---|---|---|
| **Being a Leader vs Being Administrative** | **Leadership**<br>· Inspirational<br>· Personal<br>· Providing guidance<br>· Modeling the desired future<br>· Demonstrating clear values | **Administrative:**<br>· Detail-focused<br>· Pragmatic<br>· Coordination and planning<br>· Keeping the business running |
| **Pursuing Excellence vs Allowing Mediocrity** | **Excellence:**<br>· Inspired values<br>· "Go for the Gold"<br>· Finding valuable meaning in the change<br>· Open to refinements<br>· Encouraging people's best | **Mediocrity:**<br>· "Good enough"<br>· Mundane<br>· Bored |

# Chapter 8

## It's All About Team

*"We may have all come on different ships, but we're in the same boat now."*
- Martin Luther King Jr.

In this chapter, we're going to look at the factors that make some workplace teams fly, and others fail… we're going to look at ways to nurture new teams, how to navigate some of the inevitable problems, and finally, how to say goodbye.

My first offshore sailing experience was all about team. O.K. it was all family-a family team. This team was made up of my husband and me, our three almost-grown children, and my husband's brother. We had a pretty clear goal in mind. Get this 60-foot sailboat safely home to Victoria, British Columbia, from Fort Lauderdale, Florida. It was one of the most trying adventures of my life, and the most exhilarating team learning.

We left during mid-hurricane season, and with the help of a weather router, managed to outrun some (not all) of the nasty storms. Every member had a distinct job. My husband, captain; our daughter, navigator and first mate; our oldest son, navigator and supplier of fish; my brother-in-law, navigator and electronics and communications engineer; youngest son, videographer and entertainer; and I, the job of cook and provisioner. In addition to these primary roles, we all rotated four-hour watches in pairs. We could not have done this trip without all of these important roles filled, and when my youngest son and I left the voyage after transiting the Panama Canal, the four remaining team members were left to continue the journey. And what a journey they completed! When they arrived in Victoria, British Columbia after two months and over 6000 nautical miles, a "mother of all parties" awaited them, and the crew joked about how they walked around together for the first few hours, never more than a few feet from one another. After over two months together, and an unparalleled life experience, they were virtually joined at the hip. We had set out to accomplish what felt like a daunting undertaking, and we had succeeded.

My leaving the journey half-way left an indelible impact on my sense of accomplishment, and it haunted me for a very long time. What I came to realize after some reflection was that teams can accomplish amazing things, even when the original team is broken up and tasks are redistributed. What I came to realize is that my role ashore for the second half of the trip was equally important, as supporter, party organizer and morale booster. One thing was clear: the voyage needed someone to do laundry and a communications expert and navigators as much as it needed a captain. It needed a cool head, it needed a "go getter," it needed a joker, it needed a planner, it needed someone with bravado and someone to say out loud exactly when things were getting too scary. One person cannot fill all these roles, and that is the essence of team. People come together, each with different strengths and weaknesses, and truly special experiences are created when this sense of team synergy is present.

"Teamwork," you may be thinking right now, and gagging. Certainly, it is one of the most over-used phrases in the business world. But the fact remains that anywhere you are, on or off the water, in the boardroom or the galley or the production line, it's all about team. In this chapter we'll look at different types of teams, factors that contribute to high performing teams, and strategies to promote and enhance team development.

Think of the best team experience you've ever had. What made it a great team? What were the elements or factors that contributed to the positive experience and outcomes? Could you duplicate it today in your business? High-performing teams don't just happen. They are almost always designed, planned, and carefully maintained and most importantly, the members of the team are all clear about the goals and direction in which they are heading. This may be why a rowing team may be one of the best and most commonly used examples for an effective team. All of the crew in a rowing shell knows the goal (to win), they are all skilled, they know how to get there, they know what they must do, leadership is shared and everyone pulls his or her own weight. Moreover, the trust is there that the guy next to you or behind you is also giving this race his all.

Peter Drucker of the Drucker Foundation, in his book *The Leader of the Future,* outlines what he refers to as "distributed leadership"- leadership that changes depending on the circumstances and environment. Drucker describes a time when he got a surprise lesson on distributed leadership while facilitating a workshop. In this example, he had facetiously compared a dysfunctional team with a rowing crew: "Eight people going backward as fast as they can, without speaking to each other, steered by the one person who can't row." He was promptly set straight by a rower in the audience, who asked, "How do you think we could go backward so fast, without communicating if we were not completely confident in each other's competence, committed to the same goal, and determined to do our best to reach it?" When Drucker then asked who the leader of the team was, the answer surprised him. At different times, it was the coxswain, or the stroke (the oarsman who sets the pace and the standard), when on land it is the team captain and of course at times it is the coach. The leadership of the team shifts around depending on the stage or the activity in which the team is immersed$_1$.

There are many types of teams. Jon Katzenback and Douglas Smith in their essential guide, *The Wisdom of Teams* repeatedly refer to the need for leaders to focus on performance as an integral factor in developing and maintaining teams. Too often, we develop teams without heeding such good advice. By focusing on performance, teams develop that compelling motivation to improve, to reach attainable goals-or to exceed those goals, and to scope out opportunities to enhance their performance. By keeping your team grounded to its purpose, you avoid the all-too-common phenomenon of teams existing only to suit the managerial buzz word *du jour*. Katzenback uses the term "pseudo team": *A team that does not recognize any performance purpose to its interactions.* In his later book *Teams at the Top*, he warns that the most dangerous of all teams are pseudo teams₂.

So how many business teams really are teams? And what makes a real team? A team that pulls in the same direction, a team that is driven by respect by its members for one another, and one that knows and shares common goals, is most likely able to function as a high performing team. But if you really look closely, many teams are the antithesis of the concept.

When we were in Fort Lauderdale searching for our perfect yacht, we encountered some of the most notorious pseudo teams in the sales world: yacht brokerages. The title "Sales Team" over the smiling photos on the office wall was a sharp contrast to the cutthroat tactics going on behind the scenes! We discovered our yacht broker hid our offer on a yacht under a stack of papers on his desk, in the event that a co-worker came in during the lunch hour and saw what was cooking in his office.

Needless to say, when we eventually sold our yacht and were looking for another broker, we chose one with a very different sales team. Brad Baker, president of Swiftsure Yachts Inc. in Seattle, Washington understands teamwork. Swiftsure's model of a yacht brokerage looks unlike most of their competitors. All of the brokers work together in the sales department. Whoever is most available answers the client's question. There is no "That's not my contract" or worse yet, "That's *my* contract," thus no ensuing battles over territorial issues. Commissions are divided among all brokers, eliminating that most common territorial issue of compensation. All of the brokers in the company have the same goal at the forefront of their minds: take exceptionally good care of the customer or client and everyone benefits. Brad attributes the company's growth in a competitive industry to their unique sales approach. Swiftsure Yachts is selling boats in an economy that would suggest this to be otherwise difficult.

## The Development Stages of Teams

Teams don't automatically start off in a state of perfection and performance. There are stages along the way to that pinnacle. "Forming, Storming, Norming and Performing" are the well-known stages of team development first introduced by psychologist Dr. Bruce Tuckman in 1965. This model aptly describes stages that teams or groups may pass through on their way to becoming a high performing team.

The Forming stage, as the title suggests, is the early stage of development when the team is introduced to the challenges or opportunities that await them. Some companies use this early opportunity to create a charter of team values, goals, performance standards, conflict resolution strategies and other important factors important to their performance. This model aligns nicely with the previously discussed Hershey/Blanchard model of situational leadership, where follower-readiness factors may be taken into consideration. For example, in the development stage, teams may require more direction and "telling" as they begin to perform. This may not be necessary with individuals within the team who may already bring high levels of skill and competence to the table although in terms of team goals and performance objectives, more telling may be required. But in any model, teams will be most effective if they have reasonable and appropriate levels of input into the what, where, when and why.

Remember from Chapter Five that conflict is not always bad; in fact it is a good sign in team development. That's the Storming stage, and that's when conflict erupts, hidden agendas emerge and also when leaders often mistakenly step in and create rules, or break up the team, or attempt to sweep the conflict beneath the floorboards. But conflict and storming are as natural to the development of effective teams as storming is to ocean weather systems. The meteorological equivalent is high-pressure systems that only develop after "lows." Good weather at sea can only be created out of bad weather. It's a good analogy to hold onto when the storming comes into play, as it naturally will[3].

If there is no disagreement, no conflict, no difference of opinion, it is unlikely that the group will emerge as a highly productive, high performing team. Managed well, conflict often results in creativity. A leader, supervisor or manager must create an environment where conflict and mistakes are encouraged and dealt with openly. In the absence of this type of environment a team may develop what has been referred to as "Groupthink." Groupthink occurs when members of the team fear offering a differing opinion or hold back from sharing new ideas that may conflict with the group ideas, particularly the opinion of the most senior or experienced group member. Differing objectives or methodologies are not open for discussion [4]. The results of groupthink may be obvious: lack of creativity, lack of innovation, fear of disagreement resulting in an excessive cohesiveness that does not allow forward movement. Some might call it "stuck." And stuck is where some teams stay. A wise captain will take advantage of the storming stage by providing tools and support for conflict resolution. Harness those winds of change that have been created by the storm!

The next stage, Dr. Tuckman calls "Norming." This is the when a team develops their own rules of engagement, the methods and the culture that works best for the whole team. Not only how to develop conflict resolution strategies, but cultural norms, methodologies for attaining goals, role clarification and other ways of operating within the group. These norms are the catalyst for effective listening, clarifying issues, setting expectations related both to productivity and relationships within the team. So, remember how my sister was shocked at the noise levels in my office? In terms of norms, it was perfectly normal in my office, to share the fun, to discuss issues in a boisterous and outwardly engaging manner with clients; whereas this was clearly not a norm for my sister's team at an accounting office. Depending on the formal and informal structures of any given team, these norms may develop organically over time, or become a more formalized part of the team agreement.

The next development stage is called "Performing." All of the elements of successful team performance come together as teams reach this stage. For our rowing team, it's when everything comes together in the best all-out effort for that crucial race. For sailors, it's that committed drive and purpose in the fiercest of storms, and for the production team it's the experience when everything comes together to solve a mid-deadline crisis. The best of the best of team development is when confidence is at an all time high, creativity is flourishing and trust levels are solid. Teams are implementing decisions and conclusions at a level not previously attainable.

## Strategies to Maintain and Nurture Effective Teams

Let's look now at some strategies to maintain and enhance existing teams' development. This is where a captain uses his sensible deck shoes in that kit bag. Even with self-managed and virtual teams, participants need to know that the leader can be counted on when things are going right, not just showing up when things are going wrong. The old adage, "You'll always get more of what you pay attention to," is a key reminder in how to develop and enhance team effectiveness. Evaluation and measuring the right things is also imperative. Feedback and "thank you" is your next most important tool.

Let's assume a few things about your existing team:

- They were chosen wisely—all the players have complementary skills and knowledge and competencies directly related to the objectives.

- They know where they are going and why.

- The goal is tangible or measurable in some way.

- The team is demonstrating commitment to reaching that goal.

They are working relatively well together, experiencing some healthy storming, and making good progress.

This almost sets the scene to "leave them alone." A captain does need to leave them alone, but he also has to be present. He needs to be "in the way," and "out of the way"; invisible and available; focused on the task *and* the relationships. It's a big role for a captain. Provide coaching support, either formally or informally. This is addressed in Chapter 7, and is an important consideration in working with teams. Scout out the best opportunities or hone your own coaching strategies and techniques to support your team. Also, control the urge to take control and to micro-manage. Micro-managing must be epidemic in some industries, as so many respondents in our survey related comments about the practice of micro-managing. Neither teams nor individuals benefit from a manager or supervisor who micro-manages tasks. Even at the early readiness stage, when new members need detailed instructions, a manager can provide them, then step back and allow the employee to demonstrate his competency. This is even more pertinent when working with existing teams.

Focus on what is working and revisit goals and performance objectives regularly. There is a tendency to step in only when things start to go awry. This tactic may actually produce the opposite results from those the organization or business is striving toward. This is because when the focus is on what is *not* working, the team's energy and resources are squandered trying to fix problems, instead of progressing with the tasks that are vaulting progress forward.

As an example, let's look at a sailing ship that has gone aground. Jolted from the day-to-day sailing ahead, the ship is stuck on the rocks. This is both a dangerous and potentially disastrous situation and a captain and crew must act quickly. The focus must be on getting off the rocks and moving into safe waters. If the captain concentrates on why they're on the rocks, who wasn't reading the chart, who wasn't paying attention at the helm (in other words, who is to blame?) the creative and swift problem-solving that needs to come immediately into play will be seriously hampered. In a grounding situation, time is of the essence. No, time is crucial, especially where there is a falling tide. Seconds count. A seasoned and wise captain will encourage crew to feel competent, not incompetent, especially in a situation where he needs clear thinking and swift action from everyone on board. The same tactic works for a production line team. It is not about ignoring problems, but encouraging team members to fix the problems with the same creativity and forward thinking strategies that have moved them ahead to date. Focus on what is working; you will always get more of that.

Teams also need resources and supports to help them to achieve their goals. It seems so obvious, yet supervisors are busy with the "important stuff" and too often leave this detail to others, or ignore it completely. Sometimes teams don't know what they don't know, and require some coaching to move into performing at their peak levels. Coaching, described in our last chapter, is one example of support, but equally important is having the tangible supports and training to do what they need to do.

Have you ever tried to do what your individual team members are doing? Job rotation isn't just for line staff, there is tremendous value to supervisors and managers and owners to step in and do the job of others, if only for an hour or so. I once took over the front desk reception and noted how the sun was shining in the window so that the only way I could see the computer monitor was to squint and hold my head behind the monitor. I asked the receptionist how she managed when the sun was so intense. "It's usually not too bad," she replied, "Just in the mornings, it's pretty bright." Just in the mornings? Only a few hours of every day and her job is practically painful? Within a few days, new blinds were installed and the receptionist was delighted. She was pleased to have a more comfortable work space, but more delighted that someone had taken a proactive step to make it so.

Take an inventory, not a wish list, but an inventory of tools and systems and ask team members what would make their jobs easier. As in the survey section, don't ask for input if there is no budget to make changes or no intentions to implement new systems or processes. Managed well, however; such a survey may enable team members to provide valuable insights into changes (maybe surprisingly small) that will enhance their productivity.

We have already assumed that this team is committed to the goals. Individual members choose to be engaged in the tasks and they bring their whole selves to work every day. When attached to performance, recognition and thank you and rewards are also important ingredients in sustaining the high level of energy input that goes into any high performing team. When was the last time you received a thank you note? What was your reaction? While a thank you note is not enough of a reward or incentive for truly stellar performance, it is a reminder that someone noticed your effort or contribution. Do not underestimate the power of a simple thank you card! Rewards can take the form of elaborate bonuses or trips, although not often within the resources of small business. But they can also be as simple and as effective as Maureen's (Bean Around the World Coffee) annual picnic. One day a year, the shop is closed up for the day and all of the staff participate in activities such as short boat trips to a nearby island. Here the owners treat the staff to a picnic and fun and reminders about just how much employees are appreciated.

Particularly in the service industry, staff needs regular opportunities to recharge their batteries-to fill up on rewarding experiences at work so that they can continue to give back to customers. No one can continue to give their best if they never have an opportunity to be treated as the best. Treat your staff well, and your customers will be treated well. This is common management knowledge, but it may not be practiced nearly enough. In the next chapter, we will explore in more detail ideas and suggestions for affordable and (depending on your team) effective rewards, celebrations and ideas to thank your crew.

## When a Team is Just Not Working

What about a team that is ineffective or dysfunctional? How does a captain manage these situations? There are two answers to the question above. Both answers contain the word "act." Act swiftly and act accordingly. In most situations, the individuals are not the cause, nor are any one individual the cause of team dysfunction. In fact, in some cases the problem lies with the captain who made up the team! There is also such a thing as chemistry and even with all of the right ingredients and cultured and planned environment, clear goals and supports, the resulting chemistry just doesn't make for an effective team.

Let's start with some evaluation and assessment tools before deciding which course of action to take. In these cases, the captain must act to reassign and redevelop teams, starting at the drawing board, and through the use of good evaluation tools and analysis, you will gain more clarity into the team's challenges. We have all experienced ineffective and under-producing if not downright dysfunctional teams. In assessing a team's performance post-mortem, ask yourself the following questions. The answers may provide clues that will help you to begin to rebuild a more effective team.

- What did the team need more of? Less of?

- Were the team members similar or dissimilar and in what ways?

- Were the objectives achievable by another team?

- Were there varying levels of experience?

- Is creativity and risk-taking part of the culture here? How do I know?

- Did we have the right types of experience and skills to fit the team objectives?

- Were there issues over which the team had no control?

- Who controlled those issues?

- Were the appropriate levels of management authority represented?

- Was the team set up to fail? (Questions are getting tougher again.)

- Were there unwritten "disincentives" to succeed?

- Did outside influences (other departments or levels in the organization) recognize the value of the team objectives?

- Were there hidden agendas of which you were aware?

- Were team members willing but not able?

- Able but not willing?

- Were team rewards congruent with performance?

- Were individual rewards in conflict with team performance?

- Can you assess whether the balance of power and authority may have been compromised?

- If the team had met all of the objectives what would the consequences have been from each individual's perspective?

A "post-mortem" team analysis is the first action to take, before implementing changes and before setting up new configurations of teams. Whenever I was ready to interview a potential new staff, I asked my office manager to remind me what went wrong that created the current opening. This may seem an odd question, but it gave me great insight at the start of the onboarding process to be acutely aware of over-compensating for past mistakes.

In my consulting business, we had less than 5 percent voluntary employee turnover in each and every year for 18 years straight. I have always been immensely proud of our employee retention rates. But, not to rest on those laurels, I made lots of rather enormous mistakes along the way. One error that seems to be common is over-compensation for past errors! An example: I had to let an employee go due to reliability issues. In her probationary 3-month period this employee had called in sick no less than 17 times! So when it came time to replace her, I had to take off the "reliability blinders." In other words, this issue of reliability was so prevalent in my thoughts that I was tempted to find the most reliable person-regardless all the other necessary criteria. I'm not sure which is the worst scenario: hiring an unreliable but excellent worker, or hiring someone who comes every day, and you wish they hadn't bothered! I saw a sign in a linen store advertising for a retail sales clerk. At the top of the Help Wanted sign and in large red ink, it said, "MUST BE ABLE TO CLIMB A LADDER!" That former or last employee must have caused quite a ladder climbing problem for her boss. Beware of this syndrome when you are re-establishing teams after a dysfunctional team experience, or you will wind up hiring employees whose only strength is in lacking the weakness of the person they are replacing.

## The Wooden Plank

In my survey of five hundred and twenty-five employees, 51 percent indicated that they were either satisfied or extremely satisfied that their workplace was free of harassment and bullying. As employers in North America, we have appropriately shone the light on the issues of bullying in the workplace, the schoolyards, and our communities. Still, in some workplaces, bullying and harassment go unnoticed. Employee turnover is directly affected when supervisors use bullying tactics and managers and owners must take quick and drastic actions to ensure that staff be protected from bullying and harassment.

The British Columbia Human Rights Coalition defines harassment as:
> *"...conduct or comment that a reasonable person would consider to be objectionable or unwelcome. The conduct*

*or comment typically humiliates, intimidates, excludes or isolates individuals and is often accompanied by threats or promises regarding opportunities and conditions.*

*Harassment can be a single, serious incident or a series of repeated incidents. A series of incidents often leads to negative, hostile or poisoned environments that interfere with someone's ability to do their job or obtain a service,."*

Brandie Yarish at Genologics says, "Be slow to hire and quick to fire." OK, so walking the plank may be a little too drastic, but getting the perpetrator off the ship at the next port of call is essential. It's not just the manager's responsibility, in most states and provinces you have a legal responsibility to provide protection for staff (and maybe clients too!) Become familiar with the labor laws in your jurisdiction and get legal advice to ensure that your firing meets with the labor standards in your area. It's a tough but necessary part of a manager's job, that of "offboarding." In my experience, it is almost always the best route for *both* employee and employer. In the case of "just cause" in British Columbia there are several reasons an employer can fire an employee including if the employee lied on a resume and misrepresented qualifications or previous employment, or if staff or clients are threatened, or if an employee is caught stealing. It may be prudent (saving embarrassment for the departing employee) to just provide a settlement package and fire for "no just cause." This is a bit like a "no fault" divorce. Let them go, pay the money and move on. It may be the best money you've ever invested.

A colleague of mine owned and managed a small manufacturing operation. He had a particularly disruptive employee and no amount of coaching, or moving this staff to other areas of responsibility helped. After more than a year of unacceptable behavior on the part of the employee, this employer paid out a separation package in excess of the labor standards requirement. The employee was fired for "no just cause" saving the employee the humiliation of debating or justifying his actions so that he was able to move on. My colleague explained that while it was a costly move, he estimated that keeping the employee on board would have been even more expensive in the long run. In any event, and regardless of the circumstances, it is prudent to get legal advice.

What about the "problem employee" who is just annoying or unproductive? It is incumbent upon the supervisor to provide opportunities for the employee to improve. Without clear expectations in writing, and without regular feedback on improvement measures, an employee cannot improve. Review your procedures and communications strategies regarding employee discipline. If the situation is still affecting others' work and causing disruption, you need to take action. At the time they are fired, the employee may be in a state of shock at the news, and you will want to provide as many supports as possible to help them to exit with as much dignity as possible. Call a taxi for them, allow time to collect personal items, conduct the firing either at the very beginning or the very end of the day, check that they have informed someone of the event, someone who can check on them later in the day, and never fire on a Friday. Firing an employee on a Friday robs them of the opportunity to take proactive measures to begin connecting with potential new opportunities or to explore alternatives or to ascertain employment insurance benefits and instead provides them with a weekend to fester in their anger and feeling of powerlessness to move ahead. Again, it is wise to get legal advice before terminating any employee for any reason.

I treasure two "thank you" notes that I have from employees that I have fired. One was an employee whose quality of work was consistently deteriorating. Despite ample opportunity to improve, performance continued in a downward spiral. Imagine how difficult it is to fire someone who just hand-made a gift of art for you...and arranged for all of the staff sign the back. This exquisite gift was presented to me only days before the actual firing. In our meeting, when it was clearly time to let this staff go, she confided that this firing was the best thing for her. She had been struggling with some issues outside of work and her mind was not on her job. It was important for her to be seen as doing a good job. She needed the time to take care of other matters and was able to leave with dignity, knowing that her previous good work was appreciated.

The second thank you note was from the employee mentioned earlier who could not be counted on to come to work! She had been given an additional month's notice and ample time off to search for alternate employment. In this case, the fit was just clearly not right and it was difficult for her to commit to the job. This was a case of my bad judgment in the recruitment and selection of this employee.

One day during her remaining month, we were celebrating my birthday at work. This employee-on-notice guessed my age at a few more years beyond my actual age. For the remainder of the month, this employee and many others continued the joke "Don't try to guess Dawn's age-you'll get fired!" We could ease the tension with humor, the suckers from the kit bag utilized to their utmost extent.

What happens to the rest of the team when staff is fired? You can expect some major disruptions and wavering trust levels when staff are let go. With clear communication, omitting any personal details to protect the person who has left, and by managing the rumor mill, a captain can mitigate most, but not all of the damage. The challenge lies in assessing the potential outcome if the person stays versus the impact on the remaining crew if they leave. Almost always, the consequences of keeping disruptive or ineffective employees on board are more challenging to the business and to the remaining crew, than letting them move on. It sounds self-serving, but it has been my experience over the long run, that employees always do better after they have moved on. They fare better economically, better in their career development, better in their values alignment. I've never heard of a fired employee saying, "I wish I could go back to the old job." Except in cases of layoffs, where the work is no longer available, people who are dismissed are almost without exception, very unhappy in their jobs. The transition to new employment is not easy, but may well be easier for the employee than staying on board an untenable situation. See the Chapter Tools for a quick reminder list of "Fifteen ways to Love Your Leavers" (With apologies to Paul Simon).

What about you? What about the captain after such an unpleasant incident? The emotional toll on the person who is conducting the firing is immense. Not even a Captain Bligh is immune to such stress. You, who are reading this book in order to improve strategies, as a caring and concerned leader, understand that firing staff is immensely stressful. It is important to recognize the stress and to develop some coping strategies and supports from people outside of the organization.

Start with recognizing what you did right in the process, and make notes about what you learned. Debrief with other human resources professionals for increased perspective. Firing is never easy or fun, but it is necessary.

## Sailing Into the Sunset—Saying Goodbye

In 1977, Dr. Tuckman added a fifth stage of team development which he called "adjourning." Some have referred to it as "mourning" and I was egotistical enough to think that I had coined the term "mourning" as a reference to this last stage because... well, I'll explain that in a following example. My research suggests that this term "mourning" has been used by others though I couldn't source it. Adjourning, Dr. Tuckman's official name for this stage, is when the group dissolves either out of necessity or circumstance or as a natural end, as in the case of a project team. Depending, of course, on the experiences of the team and whether they hit that performing stage, adjourning can be a difficult stage if it is not managed well. A captain may instigate a ceremony that gives credence and closure to the group in order for a smooth transition into new waters. I'll refer back to William Bridges' transition management advice: take good care of endings, as it's the best way to create the best new beginnings.

How was it that I thought I had invented the mourning analogy? Shortly after I had semi-retired my business, when two of my three offices were transferred over to the new administration, I ran into one of my former staff. He was now working elsewhere and when I inquired about his new job he described a feeling that could be considered "mourning the team." This former staff had been a part of a small group that could best be described as a self-managed team. Richard Hackman, in his book *Leading Teams: Setting the Stage for Great Performances* offered this description:

> "...self-*managing teams, whose members have*
> *responsibility not only for executing task but also for*
> *monitoring and managing their own performance*[6]*."*

My former staff was a member of a very high-performing team, one that was exceptionally productive and creative. This self-managed team had achieved more in two years than I could have achieved in a decade with the same resources. A self-managed team isn't about the leader operating completely outside of the team, but this team did have a tremendous amount of freedom and autonomy. It wasn't management by walking away, but management by keeping out of the way and allowing this group to perform. Goals, values, performance standards were all clear, but frankly, they did not need me. They had the capacity and the competency to manage their own performance, and they were provided the freedom to do so.

This team's demonstrated levels of readiness required minimal direction-giving and maximum encouragement and coaching. At the time,this was a team that I had never before experienced after my fifteen years at the helm. I stood on the periphery, mostly in awe. When the time came for this very special team to dissolve, it was hard on everyone, and the former member went on to describe how he was feeling apathetic about his new situation, about his feelings of loss of "the best team ever" and how he was grieving the loss of that kind of energy, creativity and enthusiasm. It occurred to me, this was true mourning. This was a team at its end, where it was acknowledged that this experience would be unlikely to be repeated, and the emptiness and loss were acute.

With that epiphany, I understood mourning after performing. It fit with everything I had learned from the research of Drs. Amundsen and Borgen, UBC professors who have developed theory on the emotional roller coaster of job loss, but here it fit with loss of the team experience. After my chance meeting with this former employee, I found myself lost in hindsight, wishing that I had created a better closure, wishing that I had addressed the team's feelings in more depth as they went their separate ways, wishing I had shown more empathy during the transition. Oh, the hard lessons of leadership! Allow teams some space for grieving. Create something beyond a "ritual goodbye dinner" to mark the ending of a high-performing team. It's a healthy way for individuals and for your organization to move steadily ahead.

Team: it's that veritable buzz word that echoes in the halls of human resources and leadership venues. There are many kinds of teams, and they all need supports and goals, and recognition. We know that teams develop in some predictable stages: Forming, Storming, Norming and Performing and we know that their endings can be difficult. What is not available in any of the research or writings about teams are a magic formula to make teams perform at their peak. No different than individuals, teams are unique and complex in their makeup and sometimes a captain has to re-evaluate and re-design teams to increase their effectiveness. Some captains are naturally gifted in developing teams, sometimes teams develop despite the worst of conditions. The magic may be in understanding more about team chemistry and developing strategies that work for *your* team. At this chapter end there are some recommended readings where you can learn more about teams, and I encourage you to continue to develop your curiosity and knowledge about what makes ordinary teams extraordinary performers.

# Chapter Tools

Recommended Reading:

*Teams at the Top* by: Jon. R. Katzenback  Harvard Business School Press, Boston, Massachusetts, 1998

*The Wisdom of Teams* by: Jon R. Katzenbach and Douglas K. Smith Harper Business essentials  first Harper Business Edition Published 1994, Revised 1999

*The Leader of the Future* by: The Peter F. Drucker Foundation, New York, NY 1996

*Leaders* by: Warren Bennis and Burt Nanus, Harper and Row Publishers Inc. New York, NY 1985

*Leading Teams: Setting the Stage for Great Performances* by J. Richard Hackman Harvard Business School Publishing Corporation, Boston , Massachusetts, 2002

Fifteen Ways to Love your Leavers

*These tips may apply to employees who have been fired, but also for those who have been laid off or who quit voluntarily.*

1.  Never fire on a Friday.

2.  Provide an exit interview.

3.  Ensure departing staff has connected with a family or friend to discuss the situation.

4.  Listen, and allow staff to vent safely and within reason.

5.  Say thank you.

6. Offer an opportunity to connect after they have left (some of the best employees are those who return).

7. Do not discuss personal information with other staff.

8. Honor the staff who have left by offering positive comments about something they did right,

9. Don't resort to gossip,

10. Seek perspective, but don't look to others to support your decision after you've made it.

11. Where appropriate, do provide a letter of recommendation outlining the things they did well.

12. Where appropriate, have a celebration dinner or "pizza to the office" party to send them on their way.

13. Do keep mementos of their contributions including staff photos.

14. Do refer to these contributions at future staff gatherings.

15. Remind others to honor departed staff's positive contributions.

# Chapter 9

## Swashbuckling Soirees
## and Other Serious **Celebrations**

*"A hundred times a day I remind myself that my inner and outer life depends on the labors of other men, living and dead, and that I must exert myself in order to give in the full measure I have received and am still receiving"* - Albert Einstein

Celebration, recognition, and reward: that is what this chapter is all about. Sounds like fun, huh? It is, and it is also possibly the most rewarding change you can implement in your organization in terms of staff morale and subsequent retention. For this chapter you'll want to pull out that celebratory trident from your kit bag, and don't forget the picnic basket. Did you pack some dancing shoes? We're now going to explore some of the fun, but nevertheless complex issues of celebrating, recognizing and rewarding employees, and how to do it right. This is a crucial strategy in keeping good employees on board.

## Celebration

What should we celebrate, and more importantly, how do we do it right? What if business is not going well? That's the time to celebrate the past successes. What if business is just too busy to take time out? That's a more compelling reason to celebrate. What if some staff doesn't deserve to celebrate? Celebrate with everyone, and maybe the reluctant or poorly-performing crew will find reason to deserve to celebrate with their colleagues. Oh! And take those suckers out of your kit bag, as humor fits quite nicely with most celebrations.

What if I don't know how to celebrate?

Don't worry, you are not alone. Just as in Chapter 2 where we talked about the importance of having fun, a manager or supervisor can't suddenly become funny any more than they can suddenly become celebratory. But this, too, is learnable, and the important thing to remember for successful celebrations is to be genuine and clear about your intent. This is a great opportunity to ask for input from your key stakeholders. Other than some of those basic considerations, celebrations can be customized to fit for you and for your staff. In my business, celebration was a huge part of our culture. From annual retreats, to health and wellness days, to low ropes teamwork-building adventures, even a film-making day. These events were the catalyst for cementing team celebration and recognition. When I think back to some of our celebrations, I am most certain that not all of them would fit for other organizations. Every year, we had a 2-night retreat to a resort we reserved for our exclusive use. The daytime activities, with outside consultants or facilitators, provided some team learning, team building, reviews of our past year accomplishments, art therapy, mission and values revisited, and lots of opportunity for both reflection and strategic planning. But the evenings! We danced. Several staff spent evenings together prior to the event to painstakingly make up the dance music mix. The resort we booked year after year had a sprung dance floor and the rest is history. I cannot today, in travels on Vancouver Island, drive past that magical place without smiling.

Yes, we were a multi-generational, multi-cultural all-around heterogeneous group of between 20 and 32 staff. This team ranged from retired military, young people fresh out of college, university professors, single moms and techno-geeks, all on board the same ship.

But the opportunity to let loose, dance and just have fun, was the common denominator. Even for those who didn't dance! This retreat was about celebration; dance was just a vehicle we had adopted to express gratitude and celebration. If you're grimacing right now at the thought of dancing with your co-workers and employees, take heart: there are many different ways of expressing this celebratory spirit and it will take time to develop and find what really works for your unique organization.

As I previously noted about the business owners I interviewed who are exceeding at keeping good employees on board, the one thing they have in common is that they celebrate. In a variety of ways, from pizza parties to profit-sharing, employers are finding unique ways to share the booty and to celebrate.

Kouzes and Posner dedicated a whole chapter to celebrations in *The Leadership Challenge*. They discovered through their research that "Encouraging the Heart" is one of five key characteristics of effective leaders. Celebrating accomplishments and having fun are practices that support encouraging the heart. These are practices that are so foundational to effective leadership that, in fact, that the authors' subsequent book is entitled *Encouraging the Heart*. The book focuses on this important topic and highlights celebration and ceremony as crucial elements in recognizing and rewarding staff[1]. Remember that ceremonies and celebrations don't have to be extravagant events. They can be as simple as celebrating together at a company picnic. Break out that gourmet picnic basket and break bread with your team.

Birthdays, completely unrelated to work, may provide an excellent opportunity for celebrations that involve the whole team. You can create a consistent celebration tradition, yet recognize each individual on their special day. How you celebrate team members' birthdays is integral to your company's culture, and guided by individual preferences. Depending on the size of the company birthdays "by the month" may be appropriate. Some small companies grant their employees the day off with pay as an extra perk. Cake and candles are probably the most common celebration and if you're new to the notion of celebrations, birthdays are an easy starting point. Keep in mind that some individuals may not wish a public birthday so be sure to respect their wishes. Remember also, the "genuine factor," because if celebrations become just another obligatory task, they will certainly lose their value. If even a birthday celebration sounds like a trip to the dentist, find a trusted member of your team, someone who clearly embraces celebration, to head up this area. While you're at it give them a new title: "Director of Fun."

Some celebrations may be considered non-celebratory events, but necessary to mark the end of a turbulent period. This is an example of the "taking-care-of-endings" type celebration. We once had a contract that involved working with a government third party, and it started off as our company had both the "recognized infrastructure" for work to be accomplished, and the solid reputation in the field -yet we never actually did any of the work! We tried to rectify the situation to no avail, and finally attended a meeting where I acknowledged that I had no control over the due diligence of the contract (I didn't even know who was doing the work as the government third party was delegating it without my knowledge.) I explained that I wished to withdraw and told them clearly, "My integrity is worth more than a gold- plated contract." This was no cause for celebration, and yet was every reason to celebrate. There was no job losses, as none of my staff had been assigned any of the work. But there were deep feelings of disappointment and regret. We decided that a cry in our beer might be a good celebration and while we were at it, one staff fashioned a small, black cardboard coffin. We put everything associated with that contract into that black box and carried it to the pub for a proper wake. It was a celebration that allowed us to confirm our values about the integrity of our work and it allowed us all to move on without crying in our beer for more than one night.

Thankfully, most celebrations are more celebratory in nature. Create what fits for your organization. Start small, or start with birthdays or annual events, and involve your key stakeholders for ideas and input. And enjoy the process-after all, celebration is all about fun!

# Recognition

Crossing the equator for the first time is a huge rite of passage for a vessel. This milestone event requires lots of pomp and ceremony (and fun). Each recipient of King Neptune's honor is named and often they are presented with a certificate to spare them from the initiation on future crossings! A fine feast is hosted; individuals' accomplishments are rewarded regardless of how strangely the ship manages these rewards. The celebratory trident comes into play here and the experience is unforgettable for anyone participating or witnessing such an event. Somehow, a general routine email of "Good work, team, you sailed across the Equator successfully," couldn't compare. In this section, we'll look at a few ground rules for recognition. Keeping these four points in mind will help you avoid some of the typical pitfalls of recognition-gone-wrong.

## The First Rule of Recognition is that it Must be Personalized.

We'll assume that you've already covered the genuine factor. Personalized recognition is received at a deeper level. Imagine if your spouse left a note on the counter that read: 'Thanks, family, for helping me out during my illness." It would seem strange and foreign and somewhat heartless. Managers and supervisors: remember this analogy next time you want to recognize special effort. How would *you* want to be recognized? Start with personal recognition. Use people's names, not their titles. "I'd like to thank George…" is very different from, " I'd like to thank our production engineer." Personalizing recognition is the first step. It's not personal if it's directed to "the team" and it's not personal if it's for "the line cooks." What if one of the line cooks did everything *but* contribute positively to the success you're recognizing? By showering a whole team with general platitudes a captain risks rewarding unacceptable behavior. She creates the exact opposite effect to what she likely had intended. There's no mistaking the intent when it's personalized.

## The Second Rule is to be Specific.

"I'd like to thank you, George for the extra effort you took in completing the production report under such a deadline. I'd also like to thank you for never compromising quality and producing a stellar report even under such a tight timeframe." If you have to resort to, "Thank you for your hard work," you may be advised to skip the recognition all together. Generalizations make the reward's purpose ambiguous and won't actually encourage the desired outcome.

## The Third Rule is to make the Recognition Public.

This may be accomplished in many ways. A company newsletter is a great vehicle for publicly recognizing special effort. It's true that we all like to see our names in print. In addition, recognize staff individually for specific contributions at company staff meetings, or when introducing individuals to others outside the company. It will make the employee feel valued and important. For example, "I'd like you to meet Jennifer. Jennifer developed our safety procedures manual and since its implementation we have had a zero accident rate on the job." Public recognition may go beyond the company walls. Nominating a staff for an industry-related award or recognition can be a wonderful and encouraging tribute. Kouzes and Posner remind us that the word encouragement has the word "*cour,*" Latin for "heart," at its root.

*"When leaders encourage others through recognition and celebration, they inspire them with courage--with heart. When we encourage others, we give them heart. And when we give heart to others, we give love… Leadership is an affair of the heart not of the head₂."*

With that in mind, try to avoid the standard public recognition traps. "Employee of the Month" may be the most unoriginal, overdone methodology. This tactic quickly becomes insincere as, month after month, someone different is chosen. Spontaneity is your best strategy to escape these types of scheduled, mechanized, ineffective employee recognition programs.

## The Fourth Rule of Recognition is to tie it in With Values

If your organization has worked through some values clarification, made values a part of who you are and how your organization operates, then recognition has to be aligned accordingly. For example, if you state that honesty is a value, but you honor and recognize an employee who duped a customer into buying a faulty piece of equipment, you're sailing in perilous seas. Be acutely aware of what you're recognizing (especially publicly recognizing) because you're likely to get more. A captain's role here is about standing up for values and choosing what it is that she wants to recognize. At every opportunity, honor and recognize when core values are demonstrated or acted upon. If the customer really does come first, then, in some cases *not* making the sale could be recognition-worthy! Or in my example, with a competition gone wrong: if teamwork is valued, don't recognize and reward individual competitions. Recognize and reward individual contributions within a team, but don't set up team members against each other. Be aware of what you are recognizing and rewarding to ensure alignment with your goals and values.

Just to recap, the four keys to effective recognition is to make sure it's:

- Personalized

- Specific

- Publicly acknowledged

- Aligned with company values

When carefully managed, your recognition strategy will reap huge rewards. Employees want and need to know that they are contributing to the good of the company. It works like a powerful winch on a sailing vessel. A few wraps of line around the winch and raising the sails is exponentially easier. The mechanical advantage of a powerful winch is simple but measurable. Recognizing and rewarding crew works the same way; it's simple to implement, and it almost always contributes exponentially to increased energy and commitment by staff. The power of recognition raises the sails of crew morale and carries your team forward like no other tool. But the inner workings of a state-of-the-art, two-speed, hydraulic, self tailing winch is also complex. Best practices in recognition and reward programs are, at their core, equally complex. Plan accordingly, follow these key principles, evaluate along the way, and make adjustments to ensure that employees are recognized for their positive contributions.

## Fitting Rewards

Sometimes, it's the little perks; the thank you note, the coffee card, the keys to the boss' car for a day, which inspire goodwill and sustain positive feelings about work. Imagine if your junior apprentice, for just one day, got to drive the brand-new company truck? How much would it cost? What do you suspect would be the payback? Finding small ways to reward staff and promote goodwill takes a careful effort on the part of a captain, but it doesn't always take barrels of money. Sharing the booty is not the same as setting pay standards (those great attraction factors for your business.) Sharing the booty may involve surprise gestures, random acts of kindness and increased public recognition. Rewards and celebrations are synonymous with success.

You'll remember from previous chapters Captain Greg Sager, a schooner captain and also owner of Sager's Home Living, a high-end furniture and décor store. This employer has set the bar for rewarding and recognizing deserving employees and he has a unique perspective on celebrating. In just one example, a particularly hard-working employee had just purchased a new home. On moving day, Greg and another employee loaded a van with new furniture and delivered it to the employee's new home. Here was a young man with a brand new mortgage. Can you even imagine the reaction?

In another example, a young employee was excitedly describing some new flat screen televisions he had seen. On the following day, Captain Greg Sager drove with the employee to an electronics store under the guise of reviewing some items for a customer. When they got to the display of TVs, he asked the employee which one he would buy. The young man's answer was, without hesitation: "That one, right there. That 64- inch plasma, would be my choice."

"Well it's yours." Captain Sager matter-of-factly replied.

He once took an employee who had just purchased a sailboat into a marine supply store and helped her to select the best binoculars, charts, and handheld VHF radio. Then he insisted on paying for them.

Greg Sager smiled broadly as he told me, "I think that employers have the opportunity to shock someone in a positive way. It's an art form. I love doing that. I'm always looking for an opportunity to do it."

Well, if those examples aren't enough to shock you, there are more. At Sager's store, sales employees are included in a profit-sharing program and all staff is offered a full-year gym membership to encourage healthy living. Smokers are offered $1000 cash if they quit (and stay quit) smoking. Greg Sager could write the book on rewarding and recognizing employees. Doesn't it make you want to work for him, just reading this? Well, the line to work at his furniture store starts on the right-but you might have to wait awhile; his employees' *average* length of time with the company is 20 years!

## The First Rule of Rewards is to Link Them to Work.

"When I get a lot of calls from customers who have mentioned the excellent and professional work of the delivery drivers, I find ways to reward them." Captain Sager explained. "And it's the little perks too-take someone out to lunch or dinner, or invite them to be a part of the buying process for the store."

His unique perspective on celebrations involves a very clear line between work and play. And while he consistently and creatively rewards employees and creates public recognition ceremonies to celebrate great work, he stays out of their personal lives.

"*I don't play,*" he said, "*Staff are not my friends at a play level. It's business. We don't golf together. I've never been to their homes, nor they to mine. We have common denominators, but we don't socialize.*"

Indeed, as we now look at some of the cardinal rules for implementing effective rewards, the first rule is to clearly link them to work. The line between work and play is one of the challenges for many small employers. Greg Sager understands that play at work, and rewards and celebrating excellence are *business* tools. I listened carefully to his stories and realized that I hadn't had the same perspective, and at times, likely crossed the line between personal and business with some of my staff. It may be one thing to attend a baby shower party for a staff, and another to host it. There's nothing wrong with an employer hosting an event for all staff, but when it's focused on one person, and not tied to performance, such celebrations need re-thinking from a business perspective. Rewards need to be at the workplace, or a designated alternate location and they must be highlighted as rewards, not just daily departures from work.

Just like recognition, in order for rewards to be effective tools, they must be monitored and managed. The obvious rewards like pay and benefit packages were not included here, as they are seen more as attraction factors for business. Rewards are more linked to employee retention, not merely attraction strategies.

## The Second Rule of Rewards is to Tie Them to Performance.

Rewards need to be measured against performance standards. When your crew is clear about what is expected, and when they are clear that they have achieved those milestones, or key indicators of success this is the time to implement rewards. That's not meant to diverge from the "surprise" or spontaneity of rewards, just that the connection needs to be clear. Whether it's a fun day, a great departure from the norms of work life, or a spontaneous coffee party, publicly announce what the special day or individual reward is all about, don't just have it. Tie rewards to performance, but don't limit them solely to the highest performers: instead, recognize and reward improvement at all levels for all crew.

## The Third Rule of Rewards is Don't Wait for the Big Breakthroughs to Reward Staff.

It's the small successes and the individual or team improvements that warrant rewards, not just the breakthroughs or when targets are blown out of the water. Sometimes, it's when a team is struggling that they most need rewards. Investigate, get out your magnifying glass and find out what *is* working. It's all too easy to find what's not working but if you can concentrate and focus on movement toward targeted goals or behaviors that support company values, you're on the right track. Reward your champions and encourage and support those who are not there yet. By rewarding improvement you will set the stage for continued improvement and that's how business grows. Celebrate regularly with the whole team, so that those who may be struggling experience the goodwill and light hearted activities that fuel commitment and engagement.

## The Fourth Rule of Rewards is to Align Rewards with Company Values.

If your company prides itself for its green practices, and then rewards employees with a new Hummer or a half a forest of paper products, you're sending the wrong message. Create an enviro-day instead. If you're a blue company who takes social responsibility to heart, and all of your rewards are 100 percent employee-centered, it's still the wrong message. In this case you might want to consider a supporting a volunteer rewards program. If family-friendly practices are at your core, maybe a reward program that pays for child care when staff have to be out of town. Your rewards programs are not just about employee retention. Rewards are also a part of your brand, so ensure alignment with what it is you are representing to ensure consistent branding.

## The Fifth Rule of Rewards is Be Creative and Have Fun.

Rewards that fit with the culture of your organization can be as creative or unique as your team. Take a look at the list of ideas in chapter tools. Develop a budget and determine time resources available, then invite your key stakeholders to help choose some rewards that would be fitting for your particular crew. Be creative with ideas, and encourage staff feedback on any rewards program you implement.

Consider the five rules in implementing new rewards or in evaluating your current system:

- Link them to work

- Tie them to performance

- Don't wait for the big breakthroughs

- Align rewards with company values

- Be creative and have fun

There is enormous joy for most captains in sharing the booty and bestowing rewards upon the crew. Celebrations, be they a dance, a birthday gathering, or an awards ceremony will fill your sails with goodwill and increased employee engagement. Recognition will encourage the hearts of the crew and warm the heart of the captain and rewards will increase productivity and success. All three together, celebration, recognition and rewards, will turn your journey from a task-oriented humdrum sail from point A to point B into an enjoyable and fun adventure!

## Chapter Tools

## 50 Ways to Say Thanks to Your Employees:

1. **Personalized thank you notes**. A handwritten note speaks volumes about gratitude and caring.

2. **Gift certificate** related to an individual's interests: art supply store, golf equipment store, ski pass, pet supply store, hardware store, bookstore, home décor, etc.

3. **Coffee passes.** Purchase a punch card or certificate for staff's favorite coffee take-out.

4. **Personalized gift bag.** Include a magazine related to staff interest, a large chocolate bar or fruit chews, a restaurant gift certificate and a small package of coffee or hot chocolate or teabags.

5. **Photos:** Enlarge a photo of each staff on the job. We rarely have photos of ourselves at work. A large photo of the individual, autographed with "Thanks" and your signature would be treasured.

6. **Pizza lunch.** Have pizza delivered to the office during the lunch break and invite everyone to enjoy. Stagger the lunch times and mix it up so that staff has a unique opportunity to mix with colleagues who normally take a different time for a break.

7. **Go for a picnic.** Leave the office or production line. Either hire a substitute or do this on two days with half the staff on each. Have a caterer prepare a huge picnic basket and head off to a picturesque location.

8. **Morning coffee surprise.** Have a caterer deliver exquisite pastries, fresh fruit and gourmet coffee just in time for coffee break.

9. **Attach a staff's name to a product.** Name items on your restaurant menu, or processes or products after staff who have contributed, i.e. "Joel's Apple Pie" or "Angela's Safety Checklist" or "Gordon's Clips."

10. **Take out an ad** in the newspaper to celebrate someone's special accomplishment. For example: "At XYZ Company we're proud to announce that Sam Smith has received an honors MBA degree."

11. **A day off with pay.** Surprise a high-performing employee with a day off with pay in the middle of the week.

12. **Take an employee to breakfast or lunch.** This one-on-one time is precious for giver and receiver.

13. **Spa gift certificate.** Provide a spa certificate and award time off work to attend.

14. **Gas card or certificate.** Reward that hard-working employee who commutes long distances to get to work.

15. **Concierge service.** Provide a gift certificate for the employee who doesn't have time to run personal errands.

16. **Monthly gym passes.** For the whole crew, or for an individual.

17. **Leave an hour early pass.** Provide a certificate that allows an employee to leave an hour early on the day of their choice.

18. **Take-out dinner.** Provide a certificate for ethnic food or employee's favorite restaurant for a Friday night take-out.

19. **New tools.** Put a ribbon and a personalized card on a new printer, drill, or a fountain pen that will help your crew do their job.

20. **Community garden project.** Purchase seeds or plants and pay staff to donate a day of volunteering at a community garden project.

21. **Team building event.** Go sailing! Or white water rafting, or fishing, or play Monopoly, anything that involves all team members in an activity away from the workplace.

22. **New uniforms**. Or a certificate to a uniform shop.

23. **Certificate for an evening college course**, related to staff interests.

24. **Tickets to a concert.** When an employee expresses interest in a particular play, or music event, surprise them with two tickets.

25. **A wall plaque,** or poster, something related to the employee's contributions at work. For example, a team leader would appreciate a motivational "teamwork" poster.

26. **Coffee mugs,** with company logo and individual names.

27. **Waive coffee fees for a month**. If staff is contributing to a coffee fund, have a "month of coffee on me" reward.

28. **Volunteer Time,** for staff that provide volunteer work in the community, reward with time off on a regular basis to participate in the community.

29. **Child care reimbursement.** Pay staff childcare costs when staff has to be out of town for work.

30. **Random acts of kindness.** Provide staff with transit tickets, small amounts of cash, book of free coffee certificates etc. and set them loose in the community to perform random acts of kindness.

31. **Wild Ideas Party**. Host a catered event that encourages creative brainstorming and problem-solving. Give prizes to the most creative ideas.

32. **Medal ceremony.** Engrave a medal for each employee with one word that describes their special contribution to the workplace. Hold a ceremony and present the medals.

33. **Wellness Day**. Set aside a whole day and invite experts in to address wellness issues. Provide sample products and a mobile chair massage option.

34. **Eco-Friendly Day.** Same as above. Invite experts in to discuss ways to make your workplace more earth-friendly. Provide sample products and prizes for new ideas that may be implemented.

35. **Boss for the Day.** Invite an employee to take on your job for a day, while you do their job for the day. Share and debrief with all staff.

36. **Make a film.** Get your budding videographers to create a fun video of a day in the life of your company. Give everyone a role, allow for Academy Award-winning performances from all of your stars.

37. **T-Shirts.** Create a fun T-shirt contest with company logo, cartoons or caricatures. Award prizes for the best in show.

38. **Book Club.** This idea from Brandie Yarish at Genologics Inc. Implement a lunch hour book discussion group, and purchase the first ten books with input from staff.

39. **Spouse or Significant Other Recognition Night.** Host an evening that celebrates the contributions of spouse of other family, or "significant other" supports for employees.

40. **Bring Your Child to Work Day.** Encourage staff to participate in an annual bring-your-child-to-work day. Double check safety procedures and review them with employees prior to the event.

41. **Bring Your Pet to Work Day.** Same as above, where appropriate. Check out pet-compatibility issues and allergy alerts prior to approving this one. A "dog walk afternoon" may be an appropriate alternative.

42. **Show Off Day.** An adult version of Show-and-Tell! Invite staff to bring in something from home that they are proud of. It may

be a piece of furniture they've built, a photo of the new deck they built; an auto they've restored; a quilt they have made, a scrapbook of travels; their child's baseball trophy, anything goes. Set up a designated area with time slots for each contributor to describe his project.

43. **Certificate of Achievement.** Create a certificate to acknowledge the specific staff achievement. Frame it and present it at a staff meeting.

44. **Baby Photo Contest.** This idea from Jennifer at Cold Star Freight. Invite staff to post their baby photos and have a contest to match photo with each staff.

45. **Flowers.** Never underestimate the value of a well-timed bouquet placed on an employee's desk.

46. **Day in the Soup Kitchen.** Arrange with a local charity to donate the food, and staff time to assist in the preparation of meals for the needy.

47. **Just Because Gift.** Similar to Greg Sager's examples, listen to employee yearnings and present them with a surprise gift. It doesn't need to be large or expensive, just an indication that you heard them.

48. **Magazine Subscription.** Surprise an employee with a magazine subscription, related to industry you work in, or employee's special interest.

49. **Goodwill Day.** Purchase a bag full of dollar store fun items. Draw names, and have each staff acknowledge the person whose name they have drawn by presenting them with one of the gifts and describing how it fits for that person. Donate the items to a shelter at the end of the day.

50. **One Person's Junk, Another's Treasure.** Have a "Bring in Your One Piece of Junk" day. Auction off each piece and donate proceeds to an agreed-upon charity.

# Chapter 10

## Captain's Orders—An Action Plan

*"To reach the port of success, we must sail; sometimes with the wind, and sometimes against it, but we must sail, not drift or lie at anchor."*
                                                            - Oliver Wendell Holmes

As captain, you must differentiate between knowing and doing. That's the goal of this chapter: to provide you with an action plan that will help implement some of the ideas from the rest of the book. As the quote above suggests, now is the time to sail, not drift or lie at anchor.

Look at the action plan as a map of your journey. Carefully plot out the course and develop clarity on where you want to go, and just what route you will take. Knowing where you are now, where you want to be, and how you will get there, is the focus of this chapter. In the following pages, we will have a look at how (and why) to get going on these items:

- Determine where you are now with regards to your employee retention matters.

- Set new employee retention goals.

- Discover your strengths, values and personal characteristics.

- Connect with a trusted colleague or employee and solicit help.

- Keep a journal of your learning.

- Remove barriers to productivity.

- Measure results and reset your waypoints.

- Celebrate!

## First Things First—Taking Inventory

If you don't know where you are, you can't set the course to your next destination. In this first section, let's look at a simple employee turnover calculation and then assess where your satisfaction level stands regarding current employee retention rates.

Take the number of avoidable (voluntary) staff departures. Divide by the average number of employees during the same time period.

Example: Jan 1, 2008 to December 31, 2008

In this one year period:

12 voluntary exits divided by 75 average number of employees = **16 percent voluntary turnover.**

A one-year time frame is just an example as this will give you a snapshot of employee turnover that may include seasonal or other factors affecting turnover.

Measuring employee retention may be simple mathematically but the issues behind the formula can be very complex. Reasons for poor employee retention rates may be attributed to anything from poor onboarding strategies and actions to natural attrition due to medical or maternity leave. It's good to remember, too, that some separations are good for the company or may be linked to economic factors resulting in layoffs. For internal uses, it may be best to focus on voluntary separations as a basic measuring formula. Voluntary separations exclude situations where layoffs are due to economic pressures, changes in company direction or for medical or maternity/paternity leaves or firings.

Check with your industry associations or colleagues in similar businesses to get a sense of expected turnover. But remember that while industry comparisons may be valuable, others may be using different formulas based on some or none of the above reasons for employee exits. What is important is your *own* perception of your turnover rate for your business.

On a Scale of 1 to 5, where are you now in your level of satisfaction with your employee retention rate?

| 1 | 2 | 3 | 4 | 5 |
|---|---|---|---|---|
| Very Dissatisfied | Dissatisfied | Neutral | Satisfied | Very Satisfied |

Once you are clear about where you are now, it's time to look at where to go from here. Where is your level of satisfaction? Where would you like it to be? How are you going to get there? Well, like most things in life, setting goals is a great way to get your ship pointed in the right direction.

What will improvement look like to you?

_____

_____

_____

_____

_____

How will you know that things are improving?

_____

_____

_____

_____

_____

## Set Employee Retention Goals:

You may have determined after reviewing your current rate of voluntary exits that your attrition rate is higher than anticipated due to medical or retirement factors. But if it appears that an inordinate number of crew are jumping ship for other reasons, here's where focusing on retention issues and setting some benchmarks for improvement can be enormously rewarding.

Whenever you are working on a strategy of improvement, success can be increased if the whole crew is clear about what you are trying to do. Sudden implementation of a whole new strategy, without careful communication, will not instantaneously produce the results you're looking for. Set your goals in small measurable steps, and be clear about what success looks like to you.

## Here is a sample:

*Objective: Decrease voluntary exits from 16 percent to 12 percent in the next 6 months.*

This objective as stated above would do little to help you get results. Objectives that are broken into small steps (goals) as outlined below turn a dream into a realistic plan of action. A goal, after all, is a dream with a deadline. Therefore, each step has a timeframe component to help you to keep on track.

Goal 1: Increase employee input

Let employees know that you are sincerely interested in their opinion.

When and how?

_____

_____

Hold regular bi-weekly staff meetings.

Start date:

_____

_____


Set up one-on-one meetings or lunch with each staff and listen.
Start date:                                    Completed by:

_____

_____


Create a formalized feedback mechanism such as a newsletter partially written by employees.

Start date:                                    Completed by:

_____

_____


Goal 2: Determine why employees stay on board.
Hold interviews with each employee and ask them why they stay.
Start date:                                    Completed by:

_____

_____


Calculate the results and share the information with employees about what was learned.
Start Date:                                    Completed by:

_____

_____

Focus on the positive factors. For example, if employees stay because they appreciate the flexibility in work-life balance, focus on this and increase opportunities to demonstrate that you are committed to work-life balance issues.

Start Date:                                          Completed by

_____

_____


Goal 3: Increase loyalty
Revisit your vision and check that employees know where you are going and what the future looks like, and how crew, as individuals and as teams, are aligned with that vision.
Start Date:                                          Completed by:

_____

_____


Determine how you are seen in the community. What is your brand? Ask customers, employees and other key stakeholders how they "see" your company.
Start Date:                                          Completed by:

_____

_____


Increase your "blue" or "green" factors (as described in Chapter 3)
    Specifically, implement one new blue or green strategy for your company, such as a new recycling initiative or volunteering for a local charity organization.
Start Date:                                          Completed by:

_____

_____

Ask employees what makes them proud of this company. Document and communicate the results.

Start Date:                                    Completed by:

_____

_____


Goal 4: Reward and celebrate appropriately and consistently.

Review your reward, recognition and celebration policies and practices with key groups of stakeholders. Ask key stakeholders: "What is missing?" "What's working or not working in relation to rewards, recognition and celebration?"

Start Date:                                    Completed by:

_____

_____


Implement at least one suggestion from stakeholders' ideas about ways to improve reward, recognition and celebration.

Start Date:

Completed by:

_____

_____


In addition to above, implement one new recognition strategy for employees.

Start Date:                                    Completed by:

_____

_____

The example above would require one new strategy every six weeks for the six month period of focusing on the original objective to decrease voluntary exits from 16 percent to 12 percent. Of course, this time-frame is just a sample, but may help to provide a starting point to work with objectives that you determine are relevant to your employee retention situation. No single solution will apply to every organization. It is up to you to determine which strategies and ideas will work for you and for your company.

## The Mirror Again: Looking at Your Own Strengths

Knowing your strengths will provide you with a springboard to begin developing those further, and will also help to point the direction for understanding weaknesses.

**Let's start with your strengths. From the list below, circle the strengths that you have.**

| | | |
|---|---|---|
| Advising | Bargaining | Controlling |
| Analyzing | Coordinating | Collaborating |
| Creating | Coaching | Demonstrating |
| Directing | Delegating | Designing |
| Documenting | Energizing | Empathizing |
| Evaluating | Forecasting | Interviewing |
| Innovating | Leading | Listening |
| Measuring | Monitoring | Motivating |
| Negotiating | Organizing | Observing |
| Persuading | Promoting | Supervising |
| Piloting | Planning | Recruiting |
| Rewarding | Scheduling | Speaking |
| Teaching | Troubleshooting | Writing |

List your top five strengths:

1._____

2._____

3._____

4._____

5._____

Which of these strengths will you use most in developing increased employee retention?

_____

_____

_____

_____

_____

Are there some strengths from the master list above that you'd like to improve on? If so list them here:

_____

_____

_____

_____

_____

In this next section, it's time to explore values. You will remember that the need for foundational values drives much of the behavior and outcome of organizations. What you value shows up every day in your actions, whether you are aware of them or not, so it is imperative that you pinpoint your values and then pay attention to how they show up at your workplace.

## Values Checklist

**Review this list of values below.** This is not an exhaustive list, but serves to review some of the values you may be living. You can use two colors of pen, one for personal values and one for workplace values. They may be the same, or overlap, or be separate.

| | | |
|---|---|---|
| Family | Challenge | Variety |
| Knowledge | Leadership | Integrity |
| Wealth | Friendship | Recognition |
| Independence | Freedom | Security |
| Beauty/Aesthetics | Creativity | Helping Others |
| Self Expression | Work-Life Balance | Prestige |
| Humor | Respect | Individuality |
| Trust | Green Practices | Honesty |

Prioritize your top five values below by listing them with your most important value at the top #1 spot.

1._____

2._____

3._____

4._____

5._____


How do your values translate into workplace actions or behaviors? In other words, what do they look like when they are in action? A value can't be a value just because it is so stated, listed or printed on company stationery. It has to be acted out. Take time to observe your workplace and determine where values are operating in *action*.

Values Observations:

I demonstrated _____ (value) in the

following example: _____

_____

_____

_____

_____

_____

I observed employee(s) demonstrating this value in the following example:

_____

_____

_____

_____

_____

_____

_____

List other values and their corresponding examples below:

_____

_____

_____

_____

_____

_____

_____

_____

_____

_____

_____

From the list below, check off strategies you are already using to reinforce your organizational values, and then check off some new ways you can improve and deepen your own and your crew's understanding of these values.

## At XYZ Company, We Currently/We Could:

- Ensure that we have a clear set of values, or work with employees to develop our core values.

- Utilize 360-degree feedback tools, such as the LPI (listed in Chapter Tools, Chapter Seven).

- Engage all employees in a workshop or retreat to explore or reinforce shared work values.

- Spend time observing and then offer feedback on observed values to all crew.

- Ask employees about the values that they have observed at work.

- Ask employees where they see stated and shared values conflicting with actions.

- Reinforce values through rewards that reflect work values.

Other ideas _____

_____

Personal values and organizational values usually have some crossover and of course personal attributes in this next section describe the personal attributes or personal characteristics that make you unique.

## Personal Attributes

Understanding, recognizing and utilizing your personal attributes in *how* you go about doing things is another important waypoint in your journey. One very wise statement I have heard many times goes like this: "How you do anything is how you do everything." Reflecting on this may provide some insight into how you approach many situations. When my middle son was in grade three he won a Mother's Day art contest. The goal was to paint a picture of your mother doing something she loved. The painting, in its grade 3 style, was one of me cooking. The *how* was evident in the details of the painting…there was food flying and both hands were in the air holding cooking utensils and all four stove burners were on red hot. It was a picture of how I go about doing things, usually with much enthusiasm and energy.

**Circle all of the words that describe your personal attributes from the list below:**

| | | |
|---|---|---|
| Objective | Broad-minded | Consistent |
| Tactful | Cheerful | Punctual |
| Analytical | Enterprising | Logical |
| Imaginative | Intuitive | Optimistic |
| Diligent | Energetic | Problem-solving |
| Flexible | Focused | Gregarious |
| Enthusiastic | Empathetic | Accurate |
| Reliable | Precise | Dedicated |
| Efficient | Focused | Leader |
| Positive | Fair | Diplomatic |
| Adaptable | Proactive | Dynamic |
| Aggressive | Perceptive | Good listening |
| Constructive | Considerate | Conscientious |
| Genuine | Methodical | Meticulous |
| Systematic | Inclusive | Honest |

| | | |
|---|---|---|
| Practical | Ambitious | Competitive |
| Amiable | Competent | Enjoying people |
| Gracious | Ethical | Friendly |
| Team-player | Personable | Approachable |
| Trustworthy | Profit-oriented | Assertive |
| Confident | Ambitious | Discreet |
| Calm | Cheerful | Helpful |
| Professional | Responsible | Humorous |
| Person of integrity | Thorough | Courteous |
| Hard working | Goal oriented | Self-reliant |
| Persuasive | Investigative | Sincere |
| Maintain confidentiality | Sensible | Decisive |

Other attributes not listed:

_____

_____

_____

_____

_____

_____

_____

Your top 5 attributes:

1._____

2._____

3._____

4. _____

5._____


These personal attributes are a part of your strengths.

Do you use your personal attributes to their full potential to help to motivate, inspire and lead others?

_____

_____

_____


In what ways have you demonstrated these special strengths in your workplace?

_____

_____

_____

_____

_____

_____

In addition to recognizing your own strengths, it is also critically important to recognize internal mechanisms, particularly thought patterns that may be detrimental to the process. We'll look at this in the next section.

## Remove Barriers and Increase Productivity

As part of the training for a Limited Masters' certificate, my husband completed a course in Marine Emergency Duties at a local college. The instructor, a Master Mariner, asked the participants: "What is the most important thing to bring with you into a life raft, when abandoning ship?" The answers ranged from water to flares to first aid kits and other logical suggestions. "Wrong," the instructor said. "The most important thing to bring into a life raft is a positive attitude."

Alain Bombard, a physician in France was intrigued as to why so few (less than 10 percent in 1951) people survived more than 3 days at sea in a life raft. They died of exposure, thirst and despair. To prove that survival has much to do with attitude and the will to survive, Bombard conducted an extraordinary experiment. He sailed a rubber raft alone across the Atlantic[1]. This is true for a voyage of any sort, whether you are surviving change or surviving, period- your attitude may be your best friend or your worst enemy.

So what are some of these barriers to a positive attitude and thought patterns? Some of them are so deeply engrained that it is difficult for us to bring them to light. It's extremely important to recognize the thought patterns that are guiding your life, because without this recognition it is impossible to break these sometimes detrimental patterns that ultimately shape your life, your outlook, your relationships and your experiences. Denise Bissonnette, speaker and author of many books on workplace excellence, offers a partial list of some of these **"Bad Habits of the Mind,"** and describes how these habits of the mind can affect our overall attitude[2]. The list includes:

- Dwelling on the past          Nursing old wounds

- Holding grudges               Noticing other people's faults

- Comparing yourself to others  Feeling sorry for yourself

- Blaming other people   Coming up with excuses

- Always thinking the worst   Putting down your dreams

- Doubting yourself   Doubting everyone else


Do you do any of these things on a regular basis? Any one of these bad habits may help to form an attitude that is detrimental to workplace (and *life*) progress, and will seriously hamper the process of positive change. We go on thinking all day, like the television set that is never shut off. We think and think, but we rarely stop and notice *how* we think about things. Bad habits such as the ones above can be changed into more productive habits. The first step is to become aware of your bad habits, then work to replace them with more constructive and effective habits. It takes some work, but awareness is the first step in removing this unfortunately common barrier to progress. What is your bad habit of the mind? What new habit can you replace it with?

Another more concrete barrier specifically related to business includes clinging to procedures, policies and processes that are outdated, but still in use in some workplaces. These may be processes, such as paperwork, forms, etc. that were designed before technological advances, and have been made completely redundant. Constant review of processes ensures that the way things get done, is as efficient as possible. Employees involved in those same processes are the best source of information about how to reduce redundant steps to completing any particular task. A company that encourages and solicits feedback from employees will most likely have fewer of these types of barriers in place. Ask yourself and your employees, "Why are we doing this?" and you will uncover many of these otherwise hidden barriers.

## Sample Questions:

- Is this process part of the tradition-bound routine and if so, what purpose does it serve today?

- To what extent is this level of detail required (or not)?

- How many levels of permission are required for simple decision making?

- In what ways are our policies keeping us from excelling at what we do?

- What is one barrier that you can identify and change or remove immediately?

- What are we trying to achieve?

- Are we needlessly striving for 100 percent perfection?

- What would happen if we achieved 95 percent perfection and focused on those results?

Some of these questions will begin to uncover hidden barriers that stunt the growth and innovation in a company. Small changes, with lots of stakeholder input will be most effective here. Like all strategies, start small and measure results and gain feedback along the way. An attitude or a policy adjustment may be just what was needed to propel you forward in positive ways that were formerly unattainable.

## Connect With a Trusted Colleague

Whether you find a mentor, or select a coach, or turn to a trusted friend or colleague, embark on this journey with someone who holds your best interests at heart and it will make for smoother sailing. A manager's or leader's or owner's responsibilities can be overwhelming at the best of times, but during times of change, the waves get higher and ship-handling requires more than one set of hands, ears and eyes. Taking care of yourself becomes even more important during times of change and progress.

If you're the entrepreneur, the owner of the company, you probably reached many of your goals through your vision and your strong sense of independence. But now is the time to ask for some assistance. Solicit others to assist you on your way. A trusted second set of ears and eyes will help to clarify issues, and can work as a valuable sounding board for feedback and ideas. Involve your crew. Let them know that you are working on improving the workplace, working on improving yourself and that you value their feedback sets the stage for success. But, like any improvement strategy, it is easier said than done. Knowing that improvements are on the way, improvements that will benefit everyone, helps your team to get on board and to support change initiatives. Realize too, that a certain degree of patience is required; these changes take time and consistent effort on your part before others notice changes in you, or in the way that the organization's culture is being reshaped.

## Keep a Journal of Your Learning

As part of the Masters' in Leadership and Training program at Royal Roads University, we were required to keep a running journal of our learning. This tool enables learners to engage in deep reflection and serves as a tool for reviewing major milestones and for recording those moments when the learning is profound. I encourage anyone embarking on any journey to develop the habit of keeping a journal. I learned through journaling that while I was juggling a great deal at the time, that some of the balls in the air were glass and some were rubber. I learned to concentrate on those that were glass in order to continue learning and manage all of the precious aspects of life balance. This journey is no different. Yes, journaling takes time and commitment but like any habit, after a few weeks it becomes an integrated part of your day or week.

## Measure Results and Reset Your Waypoints as Necessary

Once you embark on a journey of improvement, progress must be evaluated and measured along the way. How else will you know if you're getting closer to your goals and ultimate vision for your company? Setting these crucial sub-goals is a method of determining tangible results along the journey. Sailors call them waypoints and each waypoint represents another leg of a journey. On long, offshore adventures these waypoints provide important data for the captain and crew. At the beginning of the voyage, a navigator will estimate the time of arrival to each waypoint. Constant fine-tuning of the sails, close attention to the compass course and quick adjustments when the wind changes all increase the speed of a boat. Each minor adjustment creates a minor gain and these minor gains accumulate over thousands of miles. So too, as you approach benchmarks in reaching your goals, the fine-tuning, the small changes begin to add up and become more measurable over time. Part of a good action plan involves setting up those waypoints along your journey. Flexibility is crucial though, as sometimes, the waypoints change due to unforeseen circumstances, and must be reset or re-evaluated.

When my husband and I sailed up the California, Oregon and Washington coasts in October,2008, we had to reset waypoints several times as unforeseen circumstances, weather conditions, and exhaustion presented new challenges. A friend of mine recently told me that the new paradigm in not about surviving the storm, but learning to dance in the rain. I love this vision of dancing in the rain, because in business, in sailing and in life there will always be storms. There may well be times when dancing in the rain may be the best way to learn in the moment while moving toward improvement.

As you define your improvement goals, be prepared to measure the results. Evaluate your original assumptions and beliefs about the direction you are heading and get feedback to see how you're doing. When necessary, change course, but do so with the help of your crew and you'll eventually find yourself arriving at your original objective regardless of the unexpected route you may take. Sometimes, actually, you will find yourself at your desired destination faster if you are willing to be more flexible with the waypoints! Steadfastly sailing the same course, missing out on temporary advantages of wind shifts, will only slow you down in the long run. A successful journey requires constant re-evaluation along the way.

## Celebrate!

Don't wait until the end of the journey to celebrate. That goes for improvement strategies or for any other strategic plans. For an action plan on celebrating, determine with all crew where along the way you will set down the oars and honor your accomplishments. Most importantly, take good care of yourself through this voyage. A captain can only care for her crew when she is well rested and when all supports are in place. Don't expect changes overnight, and don't look for a miracle to appear before your eyes. You have the tools to make change, but you can only control some things. Keep your focus on those things that are within your control and you'll find you have much to celebrate! For your action item in this category, I suggest that you pick one or two of the celebration or reward choices and plan to implement them within a specified time frame.

Two celebration or reward ideas I'd like to implement:

_____

_____

_____

_____

Start date:                         Completed by:

_____

Integrating all of the concepts of developing and maintaining a core of employees who are motivated and loyal and committed is an enormous undertaking.

**Let's review some of the points we've covered in this book:**

- Be sure you have your kit bag packed.

- Get new recruits on board with ample orientation.

- Set the stage for success by celebrating new arrivals.

- Tell the truth.

- Communicate safety issues.

- Give employees the big picture.

- Set goals and benchmarks, they are more important than policies and procedures.

- Exercise pride to ignite loyalty.

- Avoid mutiny and listen, listen, listen.

- Manage the rumor mill.

- Walk the talk of change.

- Determine your values and what you stand for.

- Remember different strokes for different folks.

- Be aware of the five things your crew really wants from you.

- Allow for flexibility.

- Train and develop crew to their full potential.

- Have the courage to ask questions and hear the answers.

- Consider coaching or mentoring, for employees and for yourself.

- Maintain and nurture effective teams.

- Recognize, reward and celebrate.

It's no coincidence that we started and ended the book with the notion of celebrating. Celebrating isn't just about making people happy, it's about giving them recognition and choice and instilling pride. When was the last time you celebrated with your crew?

Feel that wind blowing through your hair? Those are the winds of change. You can sail with them or you can sail against them-your call, Captain. Use this chapter action plan to guide you, to set goals and to sail ahead with confidence and the knowledge that keeping good employees is closely tied to business success.

We knew the labor market was volatile, that the storm was approaching. I'm hoping that within these chapters you may have discovered some additional tools and some strategies to weather any labor storm, and maybe even to dance in the rain. Implementing positive change doesn't happen overnight; it is and will be a long process and will have its own challenges along the way. But ultimately the rewards of having a positive, vibrant workplace where employees are happy to come to work every day, is worth its weight in gold. These strategies we've seen in the book are applicable for anyone, in any industry with the courage to desire change! In an economic down turn, or in any economic climate for that matter, the most important resource a business has is its talented people. For the short term and for the long term, keeping good employees on board makes good business sense. When the economy turns around -as the news headlines tell us it will-these talented people will not only keep your ship afloat-they'll be the power that propels you ahead of your competition. You won't have lost them to the pirates, and there won't be any mutinies, and you'll have even more cause for celebrating with a swashbuckling soiree!

# Chapter Notes

Introduction

1   Statistics Canada  http://www40.statcan.gc.ca/l01/cst01/demo04b-eng.htm

2   U.S. Census Bureau, August 14, 2008 www.census.gov/Press-Release/www/releases/archives/population/012496.html

3   HR.COM The Human Resources Portal, March, 2008 in a survey completed by TalentKeepers Inc. a global leader in employee retention research. www.hr.com/hr/communities/survey__u_s__executives_report_**employee_retention**_a_top_priority_in_**2008**_eng.html

4   F. John Rey   *What Good People Really Cost* About.Com Management,    http://management.about.com/cs/people/a/WhatPeopleCost.htm

5   Towers Perrin *Closing the Engagement Gap: A Road Map For Driving Superior Business Performance* – Towers Perrin Global Workforce Study 2007- 2008 http://www.towersperrin.com/tp/showhtml.jsp?url=global/publications/gws/index.htm&country=global

Chapter One   - Is Your Kit Bag Packed?

1   From: Interview with Ginger Brunner, President Dynamic HR Solutions Inc. www.dynamichrsolutions. com

See also: Zemke, Ron; Raines, Claire; Filipczak, Bob. *Generations at Work: Managing the Clash of Veterans, Boomers, Xers, and Nexters in Your Workplace.* New York, N.Y.: American Management Association, 2000.

2   Towers Perrin *Closing the Engagement Gap: A Road Map For Driving Superior Business Performance* – Towers Perrin Global Workforce Study 2007- 2008 http://www.towersperrin. com/tp/showhtml.jsp?url=global/publications/gws/index. htm&country=global

3   Interview with Herb Kelleher, Southwest Airlines/podcast Jan.,2007   http://www.startupstudio.com/southwest-airlines-founder-herb-kelleher/podcasts/2007/01/19/

4   Stephen C. Lundin, Ph.D., Harry Paul, and John Christensen, *Fish!* Hyperion Books, New York, NY First Edition 2000

5   The Co-Intelligence Institute   Open Space Technology http:// www.co-intelligence.org/P-Openspace.html

6   Katherine Dedyna   *"Bullied Right Out the Door Victims Not Perpetrators the first to go in recessionary cutbacks experts say"* Times Colonist Newspaper, November 20, 2008

Chapter Two- Help New Recruits Get Their Sea Legs

1   Stephen M.R. Covey *The Speed of Trust* Free Press  New York, NY 2006   page 137

2   From: Workers Compensation Seminars, Linking HR with Workers Compensation   USA

http://workcompseminars.com/articles/2008/04/15/hr-manager---did-you-just-hire-your-next-workers-comp-claimant/

3 From: A keynote speech by West Jet Senior Executive, Mark Hill in Victoria, BC, Leadership Victoria Breakfast, May 3, 2004

See also: The Financial Post *WestJet Locks in Top Spot on Corporate Culture Honor Roll* January 30, 2008

http://www.financialpost.com/story.html?id=241844

4 "*Woman Fired is Rehired*" May 8, 2008 The Globe and Mail: http://www.theglobeandmail.com/servlet/story/RTGAM.20080507.wtimbit0507/BNStory/National/

Chapter Three – Surefire Ways to Ignite Loyalty
1 James A. Belasco and Ralph C. Stayer *The Flight of the Buffalo: Soaring to Excellence, Learning to Let Employees Lead* Warner Books Inc, New York, NY 1993 pages 94-95

2 Coro Strandberg for Vancity Credit Union, *The Future of Corporate Social Responsibility* September 2002

http: //www.corostrandberg.com/pdfs/Future_of_CSR.pdf

3 *Upfront: Dame Anita Roddick* Growing Business Online article http://www.growingbusiness.co.uk/06959143452742993349/upfront-dame-anita-roddick.html

See also: *Business Legacy of Anita Roddick* MSN Money "" http://money.uk.msn.com/guides/women-and-money/article.aspx?cp-documentid=6093912

4 The company: Odyssey Performance Enhancement Network, Chico, CA designed the concept for organizational development that links with social responsibility. Check out their website for more information and for coaching or facilitator training http://odysseyteams.com/flash-site.php

Chapter Four – Avoid Mutiny and Watch Out For Pirates!

1 Robert Hendrickson *The Ocean Almanac* Broadway Books, New York 1984 "Under the Brave, Black Flag: Pirates and Mutineers" pages 212-218

2 *Mutiny in the Boardroom* www.newyorktimes.com, November 2007. "*The Oxford Rowing Mutiny Revisited*": The Independent, April 2007. "*Mutiny in the Pews*": www.walesonline.co.uk: December 2008

3 Stephen R. Covey "*The 7 Habits of Highly Effective People*" Simon and Schuster, New York, NY 1989 page 240

4 "Johari Window" defined in Wikipedia, the Free Encyclopedia http://en.wikipedia.org/wiki/Johari_window. See also: Deborah Tannen, Ph.D. "*You Just Don't Understand: Women and Men in Conversation*" by Ballantine Books, New York, 1990 and Phil Hunsaker and Tony Alessandra, "*The New Art of Managing People*" Free Press, New York, NY 2008

5 Stephen R. Covey "*The 7 Habits of Highly Effective People*" Simon and Schuster, New York, NY 1989 pages 30-31

6 "*The 5 Whys*" defined in Wikipedia, the Free Encyclopedia http://en.wikipedia.org/wiki/5_Whys

7 Dawn McCooey "*Teambuilding and Experiential Learning*" HR Voice Newsletter, February, 2007, British Columbia Human Resources Managers Association.

8 From workshop, "*Employee Retention Strategies*" by Peggie Koenig,Principal, Koenig and Associates in Regina, Saskatchewan, Feb, 7,2008

Chapter Five – Different Strokes for Different Folks

1 From: Ginger Brunner, Dynamic HR Solutions Inc., Victoria, British Columbia www.dynamichrsolutions.com

2    Paul Hershey and Kenneth Blanchard *Management of Organizational Behavior*/ Sixth Edition   by:. Prentice Hall, Englewood Cliffs, New Jersey1993 pages 59-62

3    Paul Hershey and Kenneth Blanchard have written many books on leadership and organizational development. Their work in  situational leadership is discussed in *Management of Organizational Behavior*/Sixth  Edition  Prentice  Hall, Englewood

4    David Lennam   "*Labor Crisis*" Douglas Magazine, Page One Publishing Inc., Victoria, British Columbia  October/November, 2008


Chapter Six – The 5 Things Your Crew Really Wants From You Hint: It's Not About the Gold

1    Towers-Perrin Global Workforce Study 2007-2008 *Closing the Engagement Gap: A Road Map for Driving Superior Business Performance*. This research represents the world's largest scale study of its kind. Towers Perrin is a global professional services firm that helps organizations improve performance.   www.towersperrin.com

See also: Canadian Council of Human Resources Associations Research page "*Creating People Advantage: How to Address HR Challenges World Wide to 2015*" by the Boston Consulting Group and the Canadian Council of Human Resources Associations executive summary and details of how to order copy of this and other research at: http://www.cchra.ca/Web/research/content.aspx?f=29986

2    Additional research sources that indicate employees want to know that their boss cares about them: Andrew Rondeau presents Great Management, in an article: *Would you Fire Your Boss?* Rondeau cites the results of a U.S. Gallup Poll at: http://www.greatmanagement.org/articles/340/1/Would-You-Fire-Your-Boss/Page1.html

Steven Stein, Ph.D. *What Employees Want* chart displaying results of Canadian Policy Research Networks from the book: " *Make Your Workplace Great*" John Wiley and Sons, Mississauga , ON 2007 page 126. See also: Canadian Policy Research web site for downloadable research on social policy, job quality and labor market research at http://www.cprn.org/

3   Gary Yukl on Maslow's Hierarchy of Needs is described in the context of transformational and cultural leadership in *Leadership in Organizations* Third Edition Prentice Hall Inc. Englewood Cliffs, NJ 1994 Page 351

4   James M. Kouzes and Barry Z. Posner *The Leadership Challenge* , Jossey Bass Publishers, San Francisco, CA 1995 "Enabling Others to Act" Part Four Pages 151 to 206

5   *Flexible Work Arrangements: Helping Managers Achieve Results* World at Work from this not-for-profit organization's introduction to webinar series. www.worldatwork.com

6   *What is a Heart Attack?* Women's Heart Foundation http:// www.womensheart.org/content/HeartAttack/what_is_a_ heart_attack.as

7   Paul Hershey and Kenneth Blanchard "The Inquiry Centre", Planning Review, by Vincent Barabba and Gerald Zaltman 19, no.2( March-April 1991) pages 4-9,47-47, *Management of Organizational Behavior/* Sixth Edition Prentice Hall, Englewood Cliffs, New Jersey1993 , page 390

Chapter Seven – The Courage to Ask the Questions and Hear the Answers

1   De. Leo Buscaglia Key Note Address, Victoria, BC Elizabeth Reader Theatre, October 1977. See also: Leo Buscaglia, Ph.D. *Living, Loving and Learning*, Published by Charles B. Stack Inc, Thorofare, NJ, 1982

2   Towers-Perrin Global Workforce Study 2007-2008 *Closing the Engagement Gap: A Road Map for Driving Superior Business*

*Performance* This research represents the world's largest scale study of its kind. Towers Perrin is a global professional services firm that helps organizations improve performance. www.towersperrin.com

3   Dale Wimbrow *The Guy in the Glass,* the poem is sometimes mistitled as "The Man in the Glass" and is often inaccurately credited to 'Anonymous.' The true author of the poem is Dale Wimbrow who wrote it in 1934. * The word *pelf* in the first line means "wealth." I have seen versions where the word *self* is incorrectly substituted.

4   Steven J. Stein, Ph.D. *Make Your Workplace Great: The 7 Keys to an Emotionally Intelligent Organization* John Wiley and Sons, Mississauga, ON  2007 page 30

5   Monty Ravlich interview on CBC radio with Shelagh Rogers, June 10, 2008. See also Sanjel Corporation website www.sanjel.com

6   Margaret Butteriss *Coaching Corporate MVP's*, John Wiley and Sons, Mississauga, ON, 2008 page 102-107

Chapter Eight – It's All About Team
1   Peter Drucker, The Peter F. Drucker Foundation *The Leader of the Future.* Jossey Bass Publishers,  San Francisco, CA 1996 page 7

2   Jon R. Katzenback and Douglas K. Smith *The Wisdom of Teams* Harper Collins Publishers, Harper Business Essentials, New York, NY 1999 page 91. See also:  Jon. R. Katzenbach *Teams at the Top* , Harvard Business School Press, Boston, MA USA 1998 pages 101 and 117.

3   Forming, Storming, Norming and Performing, definition and history by Wikipedia, the Free Encyclopedia. http://en.wikipedia.org/wiki/Forming-storming-norming-performing. See also: Phil Hunsaker and Tony Alessandra *The*

*New Art of Managing People* Free Press Publishing, a Division of Simon and Schuster, New York, NY 2008 pages 258-263

4 Groupthink is described by Hersey and Blanchard in *Management of Organizational Behavior*/Sixth Edition by Paul Hersey and Kenneth H. Blanchard, Prentice Hall Publishing, Englewood Cliffs, NJ 1993 page 213

5 BC Human Rights Coalition definition of harassment (http://www.bchrcoalition.org/files/documents/QA0705R0108.pdf ). See also: BC Human Rights Coalition: *Harassment, Prevention and What You can Do About it*: http://www.chrc-ccdp.ca/pdf/h-what.pdf. See also: Canadian Human Rights Coalition. http://www.chrc-ccdp.ca/publications/anti_harassment_toc-en.asp

6 J. Richard Hackman, *Leading Teams: Setting the Stage for Great Performances* Harvard Business School Publishing, Boston, MA,2002   page 52

7 Drs. Amundson and Borgen , UBC professors researched the effects of unemployment and described the emotional processes as a roller coaster experience. Sun Raye Enterprises describes the research in their manual; Part 2: *The Emotional Roller Coaster*; http://www.sunraye.com/job_net/part2.htm

Chapter Nine – Swashbuckling Soirees and Other Serious Celebrations
   1 James M. Kouzes and Barry Z. Posner *Encouraging the Heart: A Leader's Guide to Rewarding and Recognizing Others*, Jossey Bass Publishers, San Francisco, CA 1999 Pages 23-27 and 113-118.

   2 James M. Kouzes and Barry Z. Posner *The Leadership Challenge*, Jossey Bass Publishers, San Francisco, CA   1995 "Enabling Others to Act" Part Six  Page 305.

Chapter Ten – Captain's Orders – An Action Plan

1   Tom Lochhaas, Editor   *Intrepid Voyagers: Stories of the World's Most Adventurous Sailors,* , International Marine/McGraw-Hill USA, 2003. Pages 67-86.

2   Denise Bissonnette    *30 Ways to Shine: A Guide to Success in the Workplace,*Milt Wright and Associates Inc. CA, 1999  page 70

# Appendix 1

## Survey Participants

The participants in the job satisfaction survey self selected via access at employment and career centers as well as through newsletter distributions, inviting participants to complete the survey. We utilized the Survey Monkey platform for collecting responses. (www. surveymonkey.com) All final data compiled March, 2009.

N= 525

All of the survey data was compiled by Survey Monkey Inc. and used with permission.

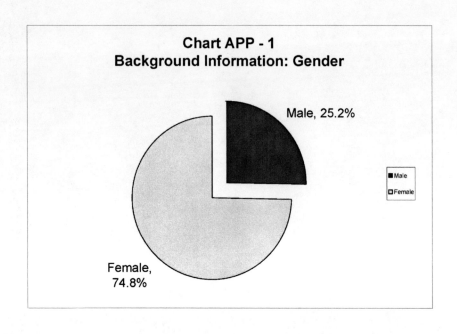

Chart APP - 1
Background Information: Gender

Male, 25.2%

Female,
74.8%

■ Male
□ Female

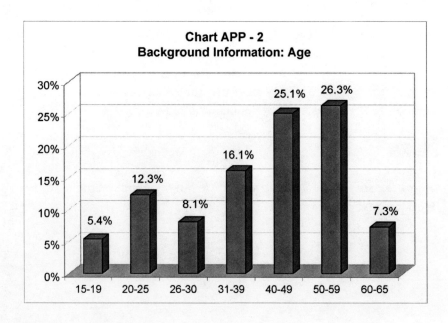

Chart APP - 2
Background Information: Age

5.4%   12.3%   8.1%   16.1%   25.1%   26.3%   7.3%

15-19   20-25   26-30   31-39   40-49   50-59   60-65

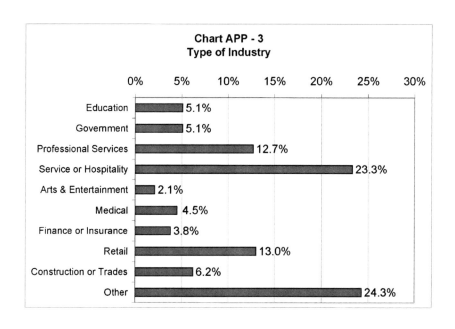

Chart APP - 3
Type of Industry

| Industry | Percentage |
|---|---|
| Education | 5.1% |
| Government | 5.1% |
| Professional Services | 12.7% |
| Service or Hospitality | 23.3% |
| Arts & Entertainment | 2.1% |
| Medical | 4.5% |
| Finance or Insurance | 3.8% |
| Retail | 13.0% |
| Construction or Trades | 6.2% |
| Other | 24.3% |

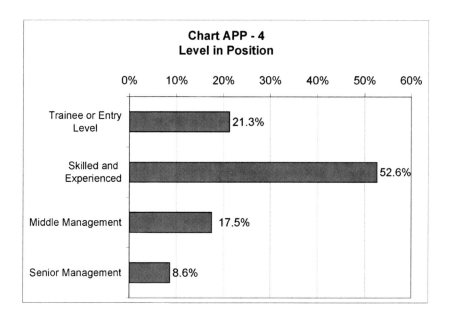

Chart APP - 4
Level in Position

| Level | Percentage |
|---|---|
| Trainee or Entry Level | 21.3% |
| Skilled and Experienced | 52.6% |
| Middle Management | 17.5% |
| Senior Management | 8.6% |

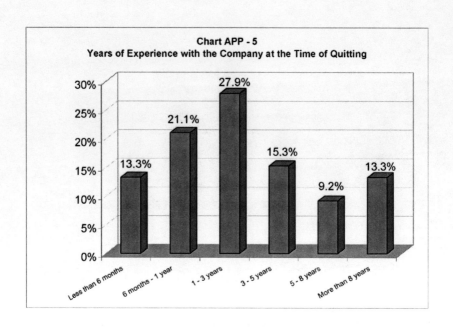

**Chart APP - 5**
**Years of Experience with the Company at the Time of Quitting**

# Appendix 2

## List of Organizations that Distributed the Survey

Thanks to the following people who distributed the job satisfaction survey :

**Norma** Strachan: Association of Service Providers and Employment and Career Trainers
**Sheila** Walker: Spectrum Job Search Centre

**Jennifer** DeLuca: WorkLink Employment Society

**Ann** Norris: Global Vocational Services Inc.

**David** McFadden: Alberni Valley Employment Centre

**Mary** Landell: Landell and Associates Inc.

**David** Burton: Career Assistance and Resources for Employment- An Initiative of Ethos Career Management Group

**Laurel** Douglas: Women's Enterprise Centre BC

**Carolyn** Taylor: 24 Carrot Learning

# Appendix 3

## List of Employers/Companies Interviewed

I'd like to introduce you to our employers and tell you a bit about their companies, and why they were selected for inclusion.

## Jennifer Hawes, ColdStar Freight Systems Inc., Victoria, British Columbia

Jennifer and her husband, Kelly, started ColdStar Frieght Systems Inc. in 1999. This company now employs 105 staff, primarily in the driving and warehousing areas.

I met Jennifer in her Victoria office and she described ColdStar Freight employee retention strategies in the most passionate and inclusive terms. Jennifer recounted her proudest moment as Human Resources Manager when at the annual Christmas party, she said she looked at her husband as they were dancing, and realized at that moment that they were responsible for all of the people in the room.

"Not just the employees." Jennifer explained, "but their families too. I never looked at an employee the same way after that pivotal moment. We were responsible to them."

**Some of the awards that Cold Star can crow about:**

**Finalist** - Entrepreneur of the Year Award 2005: Kelly Hawes was a finalist in the prestigious award by Ernst & Young, Pacific Region Business to Business Products.

Ethics in Action Award 2004: The award celebrates businesses and individuals whose commitment to corporate social responsibility has a positive impact on BC communities. ColdStar received the award for the "Community Care" for Small/Medium Business category. Jennifer Hawes organized a program to regularly collect and donate food to the Coalition of Neighborhood Houses.

**Vancouver Island Small Business of the Year Award** 2003: Awarded by the Business Examiner.

# Brandie Yarish, Director of Talent and Culture at GenoLogics Life Sciences Software Inc. Corporation. Sidney, British Columbia

"We have re-branded the whole HR system in our organization," Brandie proudly explained. "It was a year project, and at its foundation was our company vision and values. To this day, everything goes back to our foundation." Genologics has the data to prove it - with an enviable track record and rate of growth, this software development company also won the Vancouver Island Technology Award of Excellence in Human Resources – or as Brandie would describe it…excellence in talent and culture management.

Some of the awards this company can boast include:

**2008 VIATeC "Product of the Year" Award Winner**

**2007 VIATeC "HR Excellence" Award Winner**

**2006 VIATeC "Community Involvement" Award Winner**

**2005 Frost & Sullivan "Drug Discovery Technologies Niche Player of the Year" Award**

**2005 VIATeC "Emerging Technology Company of the Year" Award**

## Brad Baker, owner, Swiftsure Yachts Ltd. Seattle, Washington

Brad Baker knows a thing or two about sailing as a team, and he has applied this mindset in several yacht broker offices. But when he took over Swiftsure Yachts, he was determined to continue to develop a unique model for a sales team. Brad's team of yacht brokers truly work together. If one team member makes a sale, everyone benefits. This model is proving to be beneficial to the business, but also to the team who are about as loyal and hardworking as any employer could want.

## Captain Greg Sager, owner of Sager's Home Living, Victoria, British Columbia

It would be impossible to leave Captain Greg Sager out of this list of amazing Human Resources strategists. Greg uses the same principles in his furniture store as he did with his youth sailing programs aboard his 67 foot schooner, "*Passing Cloud*." Here is an employer that has been operating as a highly successful employer-of-choice businessman for over 30 years. The *average* length of time staff has been employed at Sager's Home Living is 20 years! That's average. Greg Sager whose famous line regarding employees is: "If you pay peanuts – you get monkeys." Captain Sager could write a whole book on employee recognition and rewards, and he shares some stories for you through his amazing examples.

## Maureen Gardin, Owner and Zach North, Coffee Wizard of Bean Around the World Coffee, Victoria, British Columbia

Customer service is probably the most notoriously difficult industry for employee retention, but Maureen and her husband, Mike keep coffee makers and servers on board their tiny ship well beyond what the industry can even imagine, retaining employees for three, five, seven years. "It's never about the pay," Maureen emphasizes. People stay with us because they are our family. This small coffee shop offers staff perks that include such things as summer picnic trips to Discovery Island, Chinese take-out at staff meetings, Christmas parties and gift certificates, and most importantly, a genuine interest in staff's well-being.

Listed by "The Coffee Crew" coffee aficionados, as one of the top ten spots in Victoria to have coffee, and with a highly enviable employee retention rate, Maureen offers her unique and refreshing perspective on engaging employees.

## Derek Emery, Owner and Gord Esplen, General Manager Emery Electric, Victoria, British Columbia

If the fast food and service industry are at the top of the list for labor volatility, then the construction industry is a close second. Employers like Derek Emery understand the competitive edge a company has in this industry if it has top quality workers. The best workers – in this labor market – are attracted to first caliber employers like Derek Emery. In a unionized company, there are no pay advantages, Emery pays the exact same as any other unionized electrical contractor. What he does to keep employees goes beyond the pay and stems from the company's four generation principle of treating employees like family, and with fairness and respect. Derek Emery is also deeply committed to developing employees to the best of their potential and this commitment shows up in extensive training opportunities offered to all employees. This company has grown from 9 employees to 50 over the past 10 years, and when you step into the front foyer you can marvel at the wall of fame where framed certificates are proudly displayed.

## Ginger Brunner, President Dynamic HR Solutions Inc. Shawnigan Lake, British Columbia

Ginger Brunner provides dynamic and innovative human resources solutions to large and small companies in British Columbia. Ginger has extensive expertise and teaches employers and managers in the fine art of managing a multi-generational workforce. The chapter tool in chapter 5 on generational communication and motivation was prepared and developed by Ginger, and I am also thankful for her personal story about multi-generational communication in action.

# About the Author

Dawn McCooey lives in Victoria, British Columbia with her husband and is the proud mom of 3 grown children.  She has over 20 years experience in her career and business consulting practice. Dawn obtained a Master of Arts degree in Leadership and Training at Royal Roads University where she is an Associate Faculty.  Dawn managed her company of up to 32 employees and was voted "Best Boss in Victoria" by the Vancouver Island Business Examiner.  She currently works part time as a business advisor for Women's Enterprise Centre of B.C., and also provides team building and change management consulting to a number of organizations.

Her extensive local and offshore sailing background and experience helped her to create this unique nautical theme for an important business subject.

Take the helm, keep your good employees on board, and have some fun on this journey. Bon Voyage.

# BUY A SHARE OF THE FUTURE IN YOUR COMMUNITY

These certificates make great holiday, graduation and birthday gifts that can be personalized with the recipient's name. The cost of one S.H.A.R.E. or one square foot is $54.17. The personalized certificate is suitable for framing and will state the number of shares purchased and the amount of each share, as well as the recipient's name. The home that you participate in "building" will last for many years and will continue to grow in value.

**Here is a sample SHARE certificate:**

HABITAT FOR HUMANITY

THIS CERTIFIES THAT

**YOUR NAME HERE**

HAS INVESTED IN A HOME FOR A DESERVING FAMILY

1985-2005

TWENTY YEARS OF BUILDING FUTURES IN OUR COMMUNITY ONE HOME AT A TIME

1200 SQUARE FOOT HOUSE @ $65,000 = $54.17 PER SQUARE FOOT
This certificate represents a tax deductible donation. It has no cash value.

## YES, I WOULD LIKE TO HELP!

*I support the work that Habitat for Humanity does and I want to be part of the excitement! As a donor, I will receive periodic updates on your construction activities but, more importantly, I know my gift will help a family in our community realize the dream of homeownership.* **I would like to SHARE in your efforts against substandard housing in my community!** *(Please print below)*

PLEASE SEND ME _____ SHARES at $54.17 EACH = $ $_____

*In Honor Of:* _____

*Occasion: (Circle One)*    *HOLIDAY*    *BIRTHDAY*    *ANNIVERSARY*

     *OTHER:* _____

*Address of Recipient:* _____

*Gift From:* _____ *Donor Address:* _____

*Donor Email:* _____

I AM ENCLOSING A CHECK FOR $ $_____ PAYABLE TO HABITAT FOR HUMANITY <u>OR</u> PLEASE CHARGE MY VISA OR MASTERCARD *(CIRCLE ONE)*

Card Number _____ Expiration Date: _____

Name as it appears on Credit Card _____ Charge Amount $ _____

Signature _____

Billing Address _____

Telephone # Day _____ Eve _____

PLEASE NOTE: Your contribution is tax-deductible to the fullest extent allowed by law.
**Habitat for Humanity • P.O. Box 1443 • Newport News, VA 23601 • 757-596-5553**
**www.HelpHabitatforHumanity.org**

LaVergne, TN USA
08 October 2009
160291LV00002B/1/P